How t

Paris Hilton

**To my gorgeous wife who, knowing my past,
still agreed to marry me.**

THIS IS A CARLTON BOOK

Published in 2007 by
Carlton Books Ltd
20 Mortimer Street
London W1T 3JW

ISBN: 978-1-84442-080-3

Editorial Manager: Roland Hall
Project Art Editor: Darren Jordan
Designer: Ben Ruocco
Illustrations: Peter Liddiard, Sudden Impact Media

Printed in Singapore

This book has been prepared without any involvement on the part of Paris Hilton in any way
Some of the material in this book was previously published in *How To Pull Women*

How to Date Paris Hilton

... advice and instruction on how to
attract and bed the women you want!

Clive RS Webb

Unofficial and unauthorized

CARLTON
BOOKS

///CONTENTS//

Introduction

Change your fortune today – no lottery ticket needed! I want you to answer these three simple questions, truthfully: Are you satisfied with your love life at the moment? Is your success rate high when attempting to date a woman and, if it isn't, would you know what to do to increase that success? If you answered 'no' to at least one of these questions then this book could be the answer to your problems.

Before we go into details of what is contained in this book and how it can help you, let me firstly tell you a little about myself. I'm 45 years old, wear glasses and have done so since the age of 11. I consider myself of average intelligence, you know, comprehensive school, GCSEs, that sort of thing and I am going thin on top. In most ways I'm just a normal sort of bloke.

So, if this is the case and I'm so 'normal', then why, you might ask, have I written a book about how someone like you can date Paris Hilton or any other woman you choose and seriously expect you to read it?

There is one answer to that and it is quite simply that from being a shy and timid teenager who would cross the street rather than look at a woman, I changed my life completely and successfully dated with hundreds of women. Using information

If you look like this, don't panic. Transform yourself from geek to god!

and techniques that I learned and perfected over 25 years (which are now contained in these pages) I overcame the pain of crippling shyness and lack of success with the opposite sex to date more than 800 women from all walks of life.

Why share these 'secrets' with anyone else I hear you say. The answer is a simple one. If you have read my acknowledgement at the front of this book, you will see I have settled down and married a gorgeous woman so I no longer need all the tips and techniques I used to use. This is why I am happy to share my secrets with you and so you will be when you read this book and start to reap the same rewards I did.

Using these techniques I managed to transform myself from a shy, introverted teenager to one of the UK's top male strippers, performing on stage to hundreds of screaming women every night. I went from being too nervous to approach a woman to someone able to walk into a room and strike up a conversation with any woman of my choosing. My luck with the ladies changed from zero to dating as many as 12 in one go. Now, tell me you would not want to be like that too?

However, before I share my secrets with you, I would like to explain why I feel this book is unique and also to explode a popular myth about the dating game.

A lot of other books available simply contain endless lists

of what the authors consider clever chat-up lines, guaranteed they tell you to get the girl. These lines and the books that advertise them are all rubbish – just ask most women and they will agree that chat-up lines work only on very rare occasions and usually only when combined with copious amounts of alcohol. They will also probably add that most women loathe them. Take it from one who's been there, they are definitely of no use whatsoever if you're the kind of guy who's too shy to even approach a girl in the first place let alone speak to her.

That is why this book is different. Inside I guarantee that you will not find one single clever chat-up line, no magic spells and no corny, eye-wateringly bad openers. Instead it contains a comprehensive system of tried and tested practical techniques that cover everything you need to know about improving your luck in the dating and attraction game. All of the information in this book has been used to great effect by myself and many others I have taught via personal coaching sessions. If you follow it religiously, then you too will see the difference it can make to your life.

In chapters one and two I show you how to send your self-confidence through the roof and increase your sex appeal tenfold even if you're the shy and hesitant type who trembles at the thought of even approaching an attractive woman. Read

Concentrate on the object of your affections

and practice the techniques covered in these chapters and like me, you will find yourself transformed You will be able to comfortably approach women in any setting or situation. Banish in an instant the nervousness, the cold sweats and clammy hands, turning previously aborted attempts into new and exciting positive experiences.

In chapter three I give you advice and tips on how to make the best of what God gave you in the face and body department. Real grooming tips that you can use to make you look more attractive together with the clothes you really should be wearing to make you look your best and impress women whatever the location. Ten seconds or so is all it takes for someone to make up their mind about you, so use this information and make a great first impression. I still follow these rules on a daily basis and let me tell you, they really work.

You will find a chapter devoted to the very important subject of flirting and what I call 'groundwork'. Being able to flirt and recognize if someone else is flirting comes naturally to some, but to others it is as confusing as the Times crossword. I explain the top do's and don'ts of flirting and body language and the signs to look for to take not just your flirting but success to the next level.

Later, you can learn how to approach a woman and get a result if they are on their own, with a friend or even in a group. I show you how to enter a room for maximum effect plus the best places to position yourself in a bar or club to increase your success. Find out how to recognize and interpret the subtle signs that says she wants to speak to you, then how best to approach her and what to say. I will also show you how to put women at ease and make them want you to be more than just a casual acquaintance.

You will find out about clever tricks you can use to impress her when asking for her telephone number and also the best places to take her and how to act on your first date. Top all this information off with simple props you can use to increase your chances of pulling together with the best places to meet women and I am certain you will agree that this book has all the ingredients to change your life and take you on a roller coaster ride journey to success with women.

The 800 women I dated were all different and from a wide social plane. There were solicitors and shop girls, lifeguards and lap dancers – even an actress or two. My techniques are suitable for all women, whatever their age or academic background. It does not matter where they live, how old they are or how much money they – or you – earn. If you study and practice what I show you in this book then you too can share in my amazing success and date any woman you want. You will find that the only barriers to success are the ones we make ourselves.

Everything in this book is laid out in an easy to read style so it's simple to understand, master and put into practice for yourself. In fact, some of the things I'm going to tell you are so simple you will kick yourself for not recognizing them before.

This book also tells my story and I guarantee it's all true. It all happened and what I describe will work for you whoever you are and on whomever you choose. Read what I say and learn it thoroughly. Take advantage of my experience and you will soon be fast-tracking your way to more success with women than you ever hoped.

I wish you the best of luck.

Clive 'RS' Webb

CHAPTER ONE:
SELF-CONFIDENCE

Counting down to sky high confidence

Today is YOUR day and I'm going to help you make it the best day ever.
Rule number one in the dating game and the most important is that self-confidence means everything. You may possess film star or footballers good looks (hopefully more Clooney than Wayne Rooney), be able to sell computers to Alan Sugar and have a body like Brad Pitt, but without self-confidence all these talents are wasted and mean nothing. If you lack self-confidence you can't even approach women, never mind chat to them. Even with your good looks, your lack of self-confidence will just make your body language appear more negative than the travel agent in *Little Britain* who's always saying "The computer says no". This is a guaranteed barrier to success and will keep women at arm's length.

I have experience of this happening myself. After weight training for a number of years I had built a great body. However, unfortunately I still had very little self-confidence. I was forever being told by many of my friends that women fancied me, but I just could not pluck up the courage to speak to them. Even when I did manage to do so, I got all nervous and succeeded only in sending out negative messages with my body language that simply said "Keep away, I am uncomfortable and not having a good time."

One big reason for our lack of self-confidence can be traced way back to childhood and the way that parents dote over their little soldiers. Let me explain. Do you remember when you were young? Life was carefree and uncomplicated, with long summer days and evenings spent climbing trees, negotiating high walls and obstacles, acting out superhero deeds and battling the evil baddies, (the gang down the street) who were out to thwart us. During these daredevil games, no matter how high the wall were were walking on, nor flimsy the branch we were shinning across, fear never crossed our minds. At no point did the thought we may be in danger ever enter our innocent minds. That was until our parents saw what we were doing. "Cliiiiiiiiiiive" my mother would shriek at the top of her voice "Get down off there, you'll fall and hurt yourself." On hearing this

With enough self-confidence you'll be pumping more than these

instruction I was therefore reluctantly forced to abandon saving the planet for at least the rest of the day, made to wash my hands and go inside for tea. This type of warning was repeated over the next few years whenever I dared recreate a similar heartstopping attempt and got caught. After a while the voice began to stick, changing dramatically the way eleven-year-old Captain Daredevil looked at the world. Things started to change. Now when I got on the wall, I started to realize how high I actually was, how far down the ground was and how I would feel if I fell. This fear of failure, a once alien emotion started, to rear it's ugly head more frequently, always coupled with my mother's warning ringing in my ears.

This new attitude resulted in my changing the way I acted. Instead of just charging in without considering the consequences, I started to hold back and sometimes not even trying in the first place, just in case things didn't go as planned. Little was I to know that this attitude was to continue.

Life carried on like this for a few years until puberty struck and I discovered the fairer sex. Ok I was skinny and wore glasses, but like any boy my age I liked girls as much as the next and was curious about them. Now, however, to replace their nagging negativity, my parents had suddenly morphed into my two brothers and my bunch of equally spotty and uninitiated in the ways of the fairer sex, school friends.

That high wall or tree begging to be climbed was now pretty blonde-haired Vicky Holder from 3T. My mother's warning that I would fall and die a painful death was soon replaced by my giggling friends' equally strong discouragement. As I plucked up the courage to approach and ask if Vicky wanted to "be my girlfriend" they all cried out in unison "She'll never go out with you, Webby four eyes, you've got no chance."

///**RULES OF ATTRACTION**//

Hold eye contact for four seconds. Look away then return to her.

This stopped me dead in my short-trousered tracks. Like Captain Daredevil, Clive Webb the budding Casanova reluctantly abandoned his quest as the last scrap of self-confidence in his pathetically skinny body slowly ebbed away.

This is the reason why so many people are lacking in self-confidence. If people tell you for long enough that you are either no good or if you try something you'll fail, then you start to believe them. I intend to change all that. In this chapter I'm going to take you through the steps you need to take to send your self-confidence through the roof. Later (in Chapter Five – Groundwork) I will go over a number of proven reminders and tips that you can use 24/7 to reinforce the new you.

The very first step to gaining self-confidence is to believe in yourself. It's so easy to think that we are great and can do anything when things are going well. When you get that promotion you have been chasing, pass your driving test or that important exam you feel on top of the world. You feel capable of anything and your confidence is sky high. Contrast this to when things take a turn for the worse and it is a completely different story. It does not matter how much people console you and tell you it will be alright, just try again, and "better luck next time", you just can't believe them as you don't really believe it yourself.

To make things easier, I first want to destroy one popular misconception that people have about the subject of self-confidence – that is that you need to be perfect in order to have it. This is absolute rubbish, after all, what does 'perfect' really mean? Everyone of us has bits we like about ourselves and bits we don't. Like art, perfection is subjective. It is just one person's opinion against another.

The next step to gaining self-confidence is to learn to understand one very important thing about yourself, and that is how other people see you. When you start thinking about this you can then progress to realizing that it's not what they think about you that matters, but what you think about yourself.

As a male stripper I stood on stage thousands of times in my career. Though the audiance cheered and showed their applause, it was the way

I felt about myself that really counted. It gave me the confidence to stand up on stage in the first place.

An easy way to discover how you really feel about yourself is to look at how you react to things that happen to you in your everyday life. Everyone of us, without exception, does something positive during our day. In turn, we get rewarded. It may be at work when the boss congratulates you with a hefty bonus on reaching your monthly sales figures or meeting a tight deadline. It could be simply a smile and a 'thank you' from someone in the street as you hold the door open or a thumbs up from the driver of that smart Porsche you let out of the side street into the traffic in front of you. On these occasions we tend to forget these 'rewards' quite quickly. However, when the shoe's on the other foot and things are not going so good and we get told off at work or by our parents or partner, it's these actions that we seem to recall and dwell upon for a long time.

During my stripping career I received hundreds of compliments from women. These ranged from my body and my dancing ability to the size of my tackle. Women gushed praise that went in one ear, circled around my brain quickly then went straight out of the other. However, when someone came up after the show and said that they had not enjoyed my performance (and they did occasionally, I'll be honest) or criticized my body while I was on stage, I found myself taking it to heart. I dwelt on that particular comment for quite a while afterwards and subsequently my confidence took a bit of a knock.

One practical and easy way to discover how you really see yourself is by making a list. Take a pen and piece of paper and write down a list of all of your talents and good qualities. Be truthful and don't be shy when doing this. Don't worry – no one else is going to see it.

Your list could contain anything – for example, you may have a smile to rival Richard Hammond, may be a hot shot at pool or possess great kicking ability on the football field. It really doesn't matter what it is as long as you are proud of it. It may take a while for you to get off the mark and start writing but, once you get going I bet even you may be surprised how many things you're good at. You may also actually discover that you are

///**RULES OF ATTRACTION**//

'Who Dares Wins'. Three seconds to make your move, otherwise she may move on or someone else will get in first.

WDW

happier about yourself than you first thought. I did this myself many years ago and this is how I managed to pluck up the courage to audition for the male strip troupe in the first place. Thinking back, I'm so glad I did.

Once you've finished (I hope you didn't have to leave the house to buy more paper), I want you to do the same again. However, this time, instead of listing all the positive things about yourself, list all of the things you enjoy doing. This could range from going to the cinema, watching reality TV or spending Saturday nights with your buddies down the pub with a few beers – anything.

List the things you currently like doing and then start to add others that you don't do at the moment but would like to, being as realistic and as honest as possible. While writing these lists you should start to see a pattern emerge that shows you actually have a lot of good points. Although you did not initially recognize them, others have and it is for these that you have been rewarded.

These other people have been giving you the recognition you truly deserve, but now it's time to take the initiative and to start doing the same for yourself. You truly are a fantastically talented person and deserve all the praise you get – never forget that.

Now it is time to do another list. This one is different from the others and should contain any bad points you think you may have. Be honest again, as everyone has them (even Simon Cowell). When you've finished, don't look to see which was the longest, just read it and then rip it up.

That's right, I want you to read it through then rip it up and throw it away. From this moment on, you are going to only concentrate on the list you made earlier of your good points and put the negative one completely out of your head.

Next, take hold of the good list you made earlier and select any one of the positive things you wrote down that result in you feeling good about yourself. Choose one and remember it. Now take some of those little sticky coloured labels they sell in stores and take out some red ones. Still concentrating on your choice from the list, go around the house sticking one of the labels in places you come into contact with most during the day. This could be on the light switch in the bathroom, the fridge door, your wardrobe handle, the tv remote control – anywhere.

These stickers are going to be known as your 'hot spots' and every time you see one you are going to touch it, at the same time remembering and concentrating on the positive attribute you chose from your list. Doing this repeatedly sends a very powerful message to your subconscious – that you are in fact a fantastic individual and, more importantly, that people really like you.

Another extremely powerful way of reinforcing this message is to concentrate on your chosen positive act and place an elastic band around either your wrist or your ankle, making sure it's not too tight or your hand or foot will soon turn blue and fall off. Like the 'hot spot', snapping this band can send your brain the same fantastic message about yourself. As the band is with you at all times it can also be used as a brilliant tool to use whenever you feel nervous or lacking in self-confidence. If this happens, simply snap the band against your flesh strong enough so you feel it and concentrate on your chosen positive attribute. Doing this will automatically have the effect of making you feel more confident, happy about yourself and banish any negative thoughts.

If you feel unhappy about walking round wearing a rubber band then simply substitute it for a gesture. Choose something simple that appears innocent to everyone else for instance touching the end of your nose (but not your groin). As with the band, at the same time concentrate on your chosen positive attribute.

This action, whether you use the 'hot spot', band or gesture is known as 'triggering' as doing so triggers your mind into thinking positively to combat a negative situation. As you continue to do it regularly you will

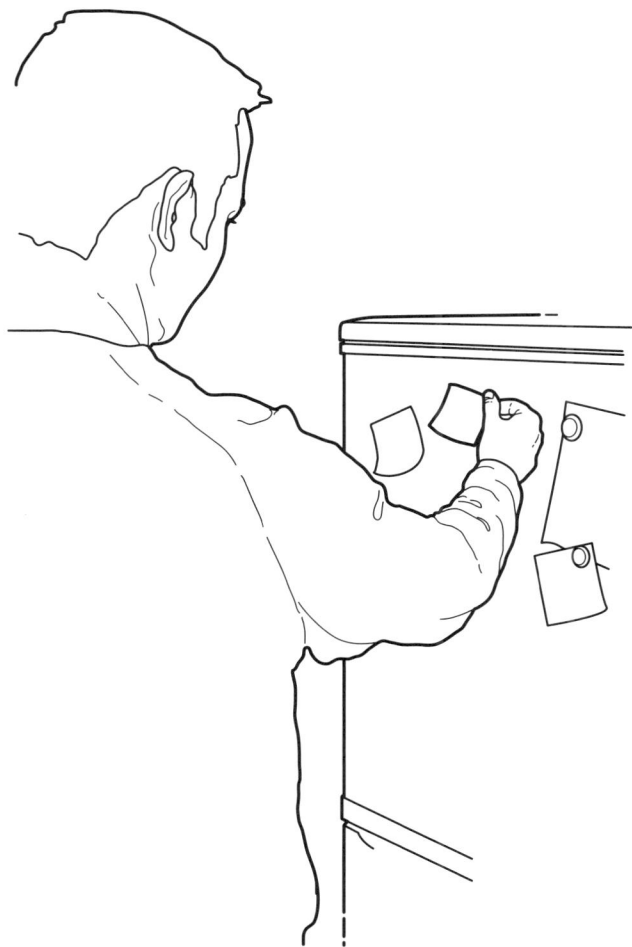

'Hot spots' – miles better than fridge magnets, especially when your fridge is telling you you're a fantastic individual

soon find it will become second nature and you will need to revert to it less and less to feel great about yourself. Due to the subtle nature of the trigger used, it is a fantastic way to boost your self-confidence without anyone suspecting what you are up to.

One of the least known but most important components of self-confidence is imagination. You can utilise your imagination to make important changes, ones that matter in your life and ones you really want to happen. The way to achieve this is by using a very powerful tool called 'Positive Suggestive Programming'.

Positive Suggestive Programming, or PSP as it will be referred to in this book, uses the power of your mind to change things and make them happen. It is widely used in all walks of life by many types of successful people – from heads of business making million pound decisions in the boardroom to athletes psyching themselves up prior to important races and events.

One great example I remember from my youth was watching the film Pumping Iron with the six-times Mr. Olympia bodybuilder Arnold Schwarzenegger. He was competing in Pretoria, South Africa, for that year's Olympia contest. The morning of the show found him telling the other competitors – including his rival, Lou 'The Hulk' Ferrigno – that he had called his mother the previous evening to tell her he had won the contest. When Arnold's mother reminded him the contest was not due to take place until the next day he replied that in his mind's eye he had already won it and it was to be. The other competitors' faces fell as he commiserated with them. When contest time came, sure enough Arnold did indeed win his last Mr. Olympia before retiring (he did come out of retirement in 1980 to win again, but that's another story). The technique Arnold used was the same as PSP and I'm sure you'll agree that he could never be described as lacking in self-confidence. He told himself that it was going to happen and it did. This is the true power of PSP.

I used the PSP techniques I'm going to describe to you on many occasions to boost my confidence before a strip show to great effect. I would sit in the dressing room somewhere quiet and start to concentrate.

I would imagine myself standing on stage with the whole crowd of women on their feet cheering, screaming and applauding me. I would go through my routine in my head, move by move, feeling every turn, mentally undressing and removing each piece of my costume – seeing the audience and their positive reaction to my performance. In my mind, each and every one of those women found me irresistible. When the time actually came for me to walk on stage I already had them in the palm of my hand.

The way PSP works is by putting you in the right frame of mind so that when you set out to do something you actually succeed in carrying it out. Sprinters picture themselves crossing the finishing line first whilst weightlifters picture that world record weight held aloft. They are all using techniques based on the principles of PSP.

PSP is one of the most powerful mind tools available to man to build self-confidence. By suggesting to yourself what you want to happen, several things are guaranteed:

· **Your self-confidence will soar.**
· **You will feel more positive about yourself and your abilities**
· **Any negative thoughts you previously had about yourself will disappear.**

The reason negative thoughts disappear is that you are actually focussing less on them. You are using more of your effort to focus on the things that you feel confident about and the things you really want. Your mind starts to push the negative thoughts into store. This was echoed when you destroyed the negative list you wrote earlier, by the hot spots you put up around your home and by the triggering used to remind yourself about the positive you. All of these techniques place negative thoughts to the back of your mind and elevate the positive ones to a higher plane.

PSP really is the easiest and quickest way to open new doors and exciting opportunities.

You may think that PSP is a skill you have to learn to acquire (or just old-fashioned rubbish) but that is not so. The truth is everyone has this ability all along, but until now it has lain dormant. It is just you have never been able to recognize or use it.

I was amazed the first time I used it and I am sure you will feel exactly the same way when you try it for yourself. However, I can't stress enough that you must really believe in it and concentrate 100 per cent for things to really happen. The first step to using PSP is to decide what you really want to change about your life and focus on it. It could be that new car you hve seen in the local dealers, a six pack to replace your beer belly or even attracting that great-looking girl you see every Friday in the local club – in fact, anything you want.

Write it down, but keep it short as it is much easier to focus on one or two choices. Now take what you've written and read it back to yourself slowly, at the same time concentrating and imagining yourself actually having the things on it. Imagine yourself driving that flash motor, or showing off that chiselled torso on a crowded beach to jealous and admiring glances. As far as the example of the girl from the club goes, I don't really think I need to remind you what to imagine about her now do I? I thought not.

The next step in the process is to relax and close your eyes – that's all. I know it sounds too easy to be of any real effect, but although simple, this next step is possibly the most important of all. Try and do it in as comfortable a place as possible where you won't be disturbed, though not somewhere you might find yourself falling asleep and certainly not at your work station – otherwise it'll be the boss doing the positive suggesting and you may well find yourself looking for another job.

///**RULES OF ATTRACTION**//

Point your feet towards her and see if she's doing the same.

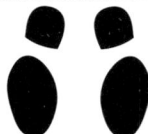

So relax, close your eyes, breathe deeply and start to picture the things you want. When you are in this state your mind is at its most receptive and you need to feed it the images one at a time, over and over again till you've thought about everything on your list. Don't worry if you've only chosen one thing, just keep picturing it in your mind.

While picturing the things you want, concentrate on making them feel as real as possible. You should picture the car's gleaming bodywork, its sexy curves and the exact shade of the paintwork. Imagine the feel of the soft leather as you sink into the driver's seat and the contours of the steering wheel as your hands grasp it tightly. Open your ears to the roar of the engine as it fires up when you push the starter. Hear the smooth purr of the engine as you roar along the open road, moving smoothly through the gears.

Feel those taut, rock-hard muscles growing daily in the gym. See the admiring faces of women on the beach as they gasp and drool when you strip to reveal your rippled torso. See the beaming smile from the prettiest girl in the club as you walk over and ask her to dance. All this sounds so simple I know, but I can assure you that if you concentrate, things really will happen.

Now that you have imagined these scenarios, I'm going to ask you to take the next step – one which will convince you that I am either completely insane or a genius. What I now want you to do is give yourself permission to have whatever it is that's written on your list.

I know it sounds unbelievable, even slightly crazy, but believe me it does work. I admit to feeling exactly the same way when I first tried it all those years ago.However, in order to really get what you want it has to be done, trust me.

Picture each image clearly in your mind and then repeat to yourself, 'I give myself permission...' for whatever is on your list. Do this five times and then move on to the next item. Repeat again for each item on the list and then affirm it as being a true statement of your desires.

Making this affirmation further reinforces your permission to have what you desire. This affirmation goes by the form of a positive statement about yourself and your desires. Examples could be 'I WILL have that car, it WILL be mine' or 'My body will look like this, it will happen'. This is an extremely powerful and very important part of the whole PSP process and not one I have introduced to make you look a right prat.

The next step after the picturing, permission and affirmation is to look and act the part of the role you are playing. Scientific studies have found that the things we look at and experience directly affect the way you feel – a simple but obvious statement. Let's use football as an example. If your team are playing like a bunch of old ladies in flippers this is obviously going to make you feel angry and miserable and affect the way you act. Similarly, watching a game of ladies volleyball makes you feel a completely different man in all respects.

This is simply because when we see happy, pleasant images our brains release hormones into the body. Studies reveal that these hormones act as the body's natural opiates, causing a pleasant 'high'. In PSP terms, every time you see yourself confident and successful your body again releases a steady stream of these 'happy hormones' into your system. This has the effect of making you feel and act even better about yourself.

Acting the part also helps confirm what you have promised yourself. When I auditioned to be a part of the strip troupe, I dressed the way I thought a stripper would dress and acted how I thought they would act. I can honestly say that I think it helped me get chosen. I also dressed that way on the way to a performance to help me get 'into the role' and help my preparation for the forthcoming show. Certain actors use this technique and often get into the role of the character they are auditioning to play by wearing their type of clothes and adopting their mannerisms. This helps to give them the edge over the competition when a casting director is choosing who is to play the part. It also helps when they are selected and are resting between takes.

Using all of these techniques together with PSP can help you to get anything you want in your life. The real beauty of these techniques is their simplicity. You need nothing more than a comfortable place to sit or lie, peace and quiet and the most important thing – your imagination.

///**RULES OF ATTRACTION**//

The flirting triangle: from eyes down to breasts or even genitals. Be subtle.

The best time of all to practise PSP is just before going off to sleep. Carrying out the techniques described at this time will help you relax more and drift off quicker. During sleep your subconscious can also concentrate solely on your desires. It is no coincidence that at some time or other we must all have had something on our minds just before retiring for the night and on waking have realized that we dreamed about the very same thing.

We have now reached the end of this chapter. However strange you think I am after reading this, I ask that you put these feelings aside and give these techniques a chance. They have worked for me as they have for countless others and will do the same for you in exactly the same way. Just remember, I was transformed from being a shy, nervous teenager to a guy who stepped on stage in front of hundreds of screaming women – no mean feat I'm sure you will agree and it was all down to PSP. Use the techniques I have described and things will happen. Why not try it? You have nothing to lose and everything to gain. So stop dreaming, start picturing and start scoring.

CHAPTER TWO:
SEX APPEAL

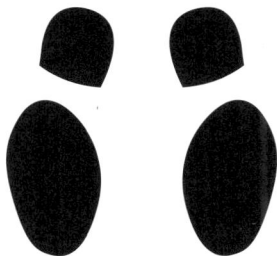

Sex yourself to the max

As you are reading this chapter I bet you feel that if a lady in the street was asked to describe you, having never met you before, then two of the words that would not leave her lips would be 'sex' and 'appeal'. Although I am confident I am right, I am even more confident that you are wrong and here's why. Out there in this great big world of ours are loads and loads of people who you would probably consider 'ugly', but who actually possess loads of sex appeal and are fighting women off with a big stick – proving that a Mr. Universe physique or a handsome face are not always needed for others to consider us attractive.

Now we've cleared that up, it's time to stop blaming yourself for all your past failures and say 'hello' to the real you. I will use myself as an example to show you what I mean: I'm 45, my hair has been thinning quicker than Clarissa Flockhart (thank goodness for Vin Diesel and Jason Statham for making it trendy) and I have worn glasses since the age of 11, yet I have slept with over 800 women. So ask yourself, if I can do it then what is stopping you from doing the same?

OK then, if what I've said is true then what exactly is sex appeal, can anyone get it and if so, how? Sex appeal is simply all about your attitude and aura – using what you have to your best advantage and this doesn't automatically mean good looks or a bulging bank balance. How you get it is again simple and the answer lies in PSP discussed in the previous chapter. Using specific techniques detailed in the chapter on self-confidence can be tailor-made to work on this very subject. After using these techniques I felt completely different about myself and the incredible thing was that other people did too – especially women.

People such as Richard Branson, Arnold Schwarzenegger and even some politicians have masses of sex appeal. You can feel the aura around them the minute they step into the room, and it's this aura that makes them irresistible to the opposite sex. Women are intrigued by and instantly attracted to these men, wanting to get to know them better. You too can be like them if you read and master the techniques I'm going to describe.

///**RULES OF ATTRACTION**//

A wink combined with a smile is very powerful indeed.

The results will be women will want to be seen with you, compete for your attention and more! This 'secret' that up until now you didn't have or even know about is called 'charisma' and I'm going to show you exactly how you can to get it for yourself.

The following techniques are designed to teach you how to attain charisma and sex appeal. Give them a try with an open mind and focus 100 per cent in believing in what you are doing. I think, no I know. you will be amazed by what you discover.

The first step on the road to gaining sex appeal and charisma is to like before, relax somewhere nice and quiet in order that you can concentrate fully on what I'm going to ask you to do. When you are in this position, somewhere peaceful, warm and comfortable, I want you to gently close your eyes and then make a mental picture of how you appear. Concentrate hard and then start to conjure up an image of yourself standing as if you're actually someone else looking straight at an image of you. Concentrate on this image and start to examine it in more detail. What do you see? Are you standing tall, with your head held high, shoulders back, stomach in and chest out? Or, are you slouching, with your chin on your chest and your shoulders drooping so low you look as if you'll soon be bent double? If you're not standing erect and proud, then I want you to start to picture yourself slowly changing before your very eyes. Imagine your shoulders starting to lift up, higher and higher until they are broad and pushing your chest out like a Sergeant Major on a drill square. Picture yourself raising your chin up off your chest, your head rising higher until you're standing at your full height with your head up, looking straight ahead and your chin jutting forward.

Picture your whole appearance changing before your very eyes and then start to imaging yourself smiling. When we smile it automatically puts us in a happier frame of mind. Interestingly, it also takes more muscles to frown than to smile, so it's physically easier to do too.

Picture yourself smiling. Watch as your mouth starts to move slowly outwards and your teeth start to show. Watch the smile get bigger and bigger, stretching across your face until you're now beaming back at yourself with your eyes shiny and sparkling – your whole face alive and radiant. Keep this picture firmly fixed in your mind while you go on to the next step.

Imagine yourself slipping a tight white t-shirt over your head and feel how it hugs the contours of your body. Feel it stretching snugly across your chest and shoulders and feel how warm and comfortable is. Look down at your chest and picture the word 'STUD' starting to appear as if by magic in big black three-inch high bold letters stretching across the whole of your chest. (Do not laugh, I am absolutely serious about this.) The t-shirt is tight against your body and the letters really stand out. You feel tall, proud, happy, sexy and powerful. Now is the time to show the rest of the world.

I now want you to picture yourself leaving the house and walking down the local high street while wearing your t-shirt. (Best picture yourself putting on some trousers as well, otherwise you will be imagining yourself up in front of the local magistrates on an indecency charge).

Picture yourself walking down the street while wearing your t-shirt, all the time remembering to walk tall and proud and to smile. It's a bright sunny day and there are plenty of people about, especially gorgeous women. Everyone is smiling at you as you pass and some women are even crossing the road to get a closer look at you. Everyone is clearly impressed by how you look. You hear them complimenting you as they pass, saying 'Who is that guy, he's gorgeous' and 'I bet he's someone powerful and famous.'

How do you feel now? I guarantee you are feeling more confident, happier and more attractive than you have ever felt before. I knew you would. By imagining yourself looking and feeling this way, you are able

Never mind wearing your heart on your sleeve – write STUD on your top!

It's not what you wear – it's how you wear it

to alter the way you walk, feel and project your image in real life. You can wear clothes that others would not dare. Even wearing the same clothes as others, you will still have people looking at you in an admiring way as you start to stand out from the crowd and be noticed.

A few years ago, a very good friend of mine who lives in London, had a habit of wearing a big black top hat perched on his head 24/7. It was absolutely enormous and if anyone else had worn it people would have been besides themselves laughing. However, because my friend has charisma by the bucket load he knows he looks good in it and the women flock round him. He just oozes self-confidence and it shows by his walk and the way he projects himself.

It is now time to take your training a stage further. I want you to again imagine yourself wearing your t-shirt. As before, picture yourself looking tall, cool and powerful, but this time you're in a club or trendy bar. It's a Saturday night, it's late, noisy and the party's been in full swing for hours by the time you arrive. The place is absolutely packed with loads of beautiful people and they're all having a good time. (I'm there, of course – can't you see me there sitting down together with the gorgeous busty blonde and the leggy brunette?)

As you picture yourself entering the room, I want you to imagine yourself stopping for three seconds in the doorway and 'framing' yourself. Stand tall, smile and lazily look around the room as if you're looking for someone. This gives everyone in the room plenty of time to have a good look at you. It's a known people's first impressions are the ones that really count and it only takes them ten seconds to do so. This is why it's important you make them really count. In addition, if you walked straight into the room without framing first, their attention could be diverted away from you onto someone or something else in the room – resulting in a valuable chance to make a memorable first impression lost.

By 'framing' yourself you are making a statement to everyone, just like a picture on a wall that says 'Stop everyone, look at me.' Now start to imagine yourself standing like this as everyone's gaze turns to meet yours. Still smiling, imagine the other guys in the room looking on enviously and the women looking on adoringly, smiling and showing their appreciation.

Imagine yourself now entering the main area of the club still looking around the room. Let your gaze fall on the most beautiful woman there – that's it, that's the one, the one all of the guys are trying to impress. As you look over, imagine her ignoring the other guys and turning away from them to look straight at you. Picture her smiling, then watch as she stands and walks across the room toward you, all the time never letting her eyes leave yours.

Say 'Hello' and then gently take her arm and begin leading her to a quiet corner. Notice how all the other women present are looking on jealously and hear them say 'That woman is so lucky, he is the best looking guy here.'

The next step is to confirm that this is what you want to happen by repeating to yourself slowly over and over again, 'I am so hot, NO woman can resist me.'

By repeating this picturing and the affirmation regularly, I guarantee that when you find yourself in the actual real life situation what you pictured will actually happen. In addition, also remember to picture this or another chosen positive scenarios each time before you leave the house. Use the above affirmation coupled with touching your 'hot spots' or using your band or gesture. In addition, for an even greater effect you should also look in the mirror, smile and repeat to yourself 'I am Number One' just before stepping out of the door. You are the best and now everyone else can see it.

As in the self-confidence chapter, an ideal time to practise PSP techniques is just before you sleep. In the pursuit of sex appeal, here is another powerful picturing exercise that you can try to good effect.

///**RULES OF ATTRACTION**//

Shut up. She doesn't want to hear about you. When she does she'll ask.

Just before bed, get yourself comfortable and close your eyes. Imagine the word 'stud' appearing across your chest in bright red, bold lipstick, using large capital letters so large and bold they really stand out against your skin. As you drift off, start imagining yourself dating loads of beautiful women. Picture how it would really feel to do this, the smell of their skin and the softness of their touch. Repeat to yourself over and over again with these images in your mind, 'I am a stud, I can succeed with any woman I want.' Repeat this until you drift off to sleep. You may well be surprised how you feel when you wake up in the morning.

PSP techniques coupled with positive affirmations are a very powerful force. Use them combined and at the next club or party you go to you won't just break the ice, you'll shatter it.

These are easily some of the most powerful techniques for actually making things you want, happen. The more you practise and repeat these techniques the more confident you'll feel and the more women will want to be around you. As I said before, using these very techniques I went from being painfully shy and a loser with women to dating and sleeping with hundreds of them. You can see that I am living proof that these techniques really do work.

CHAPTER THREE: GROOMING

Saving face – and all the other bits

Women just detest men who are:

- **More attractive than them and**
- **Who stay in the bathroom longer than they do.**

The reason women feel like this is because they see a vain man as insecure and this is something that just drives them insane. Since dinosaurs walked the earth, women have yearned for a man who is strong and fearless. They want a man like the ones described in the romantic novels you pick up and idly thumb through in the doctor's waiting room. (only because some wrinkly old granny has got her wizened old hands on the one copy of *Damn Fast Car* magazine available and is dribbling all over the article you particularly wanted to read on that beast of a car, the new 911.)

However, there's no need to panic. Don't relegate all those lotions and potions on which you've just spent a month's salary to the recycling bin and certainly don't ditch that aerosol deodorant and go 'au naturel'. To make you look your best without the fairer sex thinking you will be trying on her underwear when she next goes shopping, read on to discover the best top-to-toe rules of men's grooming. Follow them to the letter and see a marked change in your fornication fortune...

HAIR TODAY – GONE TOMORROW

If you have any doubts at all as to where your thatch sits on a women's attraction scoreboard, then simply run your fingers through it. This is exactly what a woman will want to do during that moment between the first kiss and that embarrassing silence when you realize neither of you had the foresight to pack a condom. The last thing she will want to see is her newly manicured fingernails encrusted with dirt or something resembling soap powder as this will only serve to scupper

your chances of getting any further than sleeping on the sofa with only your coat for warmth.

Choice of style or colour are not important so just remember to keep it clean. Use a daily dose of decent branded shampoo and conditioner and finish off with an ice cold blast of water to give it a lustrous sheen. These simple actions will guarantee that your barnet is as hygienic and finger-friendly as your local balti house following the environmental health officer's annual visit.

Try and get it cut regularly, every six weeks or so (plus you can always try out your newly found confidence and conversation skills on that tasty girl in the salon). Do not be too worried about keeping up with all the latest fashion trends. Golden Balls may change his hairstyle more frequently than his wife's underwear, but as long as yours is not a style that's too dated and it still looks good on you, I can't see a problem.

Should you be the type though, who drags his neanderthal-like bulk into the shower only to find more hair disappearing down the plug hole than is adorning Pete Sampras' torso, then it's time to bite the bullet and get with the clippers. I guarantee that less is indeed more and works wonders on the ladies – with my own experiences as testimonials. Avoid like the plague the dreaded combover. Raise a glass in celebration to Diesel, Kemp and Statham and ignore the likes of Trump, Coates and Charlton. If in doubt ditch the comb and get a crop.

A positive result to resembling Kojak instead of Columbo, is that one thing women love even more than running their hands through the contents of a man's wallet is smoothing them tenderly all over a bloke's newly shaved bonce. Congratulations, you are now the proud possessor of your very own solar-powered love machine. Keep it well maintained and it will reward you with hours of pleasure.

FACE FACTS

I've lost count the number of glossy magazines – and women working in overpriced salons whose faces resemble the colour of the fat bloke in that classic 'slapping' Tango advert – who insist that the only way to achieve great skin is as expensive and complex as the instructions for a DIY set of wardrobes from Ikea.

The real truth is that your skin is a relatively simple feat of natural engineering. Like the modern motor car, it will continue to look it's best with only the odd minor breakdown if you maintain it regularly.

Taking care of your skin does not require hours in front of the mirror. It certainly won't affect what Mother Nature bestowed on you so you'll still be able to reverse park and there'll be no requirement to go to the gents with half a dozen of your mates in tow either!

The most important rule is the same as the request from the ref at a Tyson bout – keep it clean. Washing both morning and night with a deep cleansing but mild facial wash helps enormously. It goes without saying, also use it straight after you have finished changing the plugs on your car or after a muddy session on the football field. Do not use soap as it'll only dry out your skin and make you smell like the perfume counter at Selfridges.

Twice a week, scrub your t-zone (your forehead and the area down your nose) with a face scrub, again perfume-free, leaving it on for a couple of minutes. This will loosen any ugly blackheads lurking and also slough off

---

///**RULES OF ATTRACTION**//

Framing. Pause in a doorway before entering.

any dead skin cells, resulting in a face squeakier than Sooty's sidekick. Never, however, choose one with the consistency of the bottom of your fish tank. Your skin's tough but no Rambo. After all, you don't want to end up looking like some extra from *The Texas Chainsaw Massacre*.

The next step is to head for the kitchen and boil a kettle. 'Tea?' I hear you ask, 'I thought I was washing?' You are, and that kettle holds the key to the next stage to perfect skin. While you're waiting for it to boil, wash off the scrub, as it's done it's job. Be careful not to get any in your eyes as it stings like hell.

Your skin should already be looking and feeling better as you pour the boiling water into a large bowl. Cover your head with a towel and sit with your face over the water for about five minutes while the steam opens your pores. When the time's up, rinse your face thoroughly with cool – but not cold – water to temporarily tighten your pores.

Once a week get a face mask sachet from your local supermarket. Do not be embarrassed when buying it as I can guarantee the checkout girls serving you have seen much stranger things on their conveyor belts.

Follow the instructions for use and go and do something else or just relax for the next ten minutes or for the time recommended on the packet (you may want to take this time to practice your PSP techniques). Should the doorbell ring, either ignore it completely or tell the open-mouthed postman you are busy researching for your up-and-coming role as an extra in *Braveheart 2: The Return*.

When the time's up, rinse it all off again with cold water and finish off all that good work with a moisturizer. You wouldn't wash your car and not polish it and the same applies to your face as water has a drying effect that needs to be addressed. Apply a moisturizer all over, avoiding the delicate eye area, blotting the excess off with a tissue. Make sure you use one with a built-in sunscreen to combat the sun's harmful rays and keep your skin wrinkle free and healthy.

It may sound camper than a field full of scouts, but don't neglect the skin under your eyes. In a later chapter we will be discussing your eyes as an important pulling tool, so let's not forget them now. They are the first part of your face to start to droop, so apply a light eye cream on the area between eyebrow and lid and underneath the eye on the orbital bone. Be gentle and only use a little (as much as a grain of rice). Otherwise instead of 'come to bed' peepers you'll end up with 'I think I've got glass in them' ones instead.

I'm well ware that a tan looks good and makes us feel great, but please go easy on the sunbed or preferably leave them alone altogether. You may think you look better with a slight facial reddening after that alcohol-fuelled two-week lads' holiday in Falaraki, but apart from ultimately creating that 'leather face' look, you're also rapidly increasing your chances of contracting skin cancer. If white is not your shade and if you must go brown, use a good fake tan or skin bronzer, both of which are available at your local chemist. A great alternative is a spray tan from an automated booth or salon. Although expensive, good ones can give you a natural looking glow that lasts between seven and ten days.

We now come to the subject of shaving – and I mean you, not her. Believe it or not, what we see as a repetitive and mundane act is loved by the fairer sex. They adore the feel of a man's smooth chin as it doesn't tickle their lips when you kiss them. If you shave without them even having to ask in the first place, then the world is your oyster as they'll see you as a sensitive and caring sort.

The most frequent question at this stage is "But what is the right way to do it?" For this I feel I must blame those men we have looked up to since we could first crawl, notably our fathers. I'll explain.

As soon as any pubescent female discovers she has hair growing down below or complains of an upset stomach on a regular basis, her mother whisks her off to the bathroom and teaches her all about puberty, periods and the obligatory talk on where a baby comes from.

Boys, on the other hand, get absolutely no tuition on such matters from their elders. When we find the same curly ones growing wild on our spotty chins as have taken root downstairs, Dad suddenly hides behind his well-thumbed copy of the *What Golf Club* monthly. This leaves you ignorant and bewildered, hacking away at the offending areas with one of your Dad's rusty disposables, resulting in a scene that could have come straight out of *Saw 3*. (Then again I suppose it could be even worse and we could all have an old man like Jim's from *American Pie*). So read on and learn how to have a peachy, toilet-paper-free jawline.

Firstly I want you to follow the example of your local curry house – do not worry if you're confused, it will soon become clear. That lemon-scented hot moist flannel, mistaken by all of us at one time or another for a banana fritter following twelve bottles of Stella can help you attain your goal. Here's how it works.

Take a small hand towel, run it under the tap and squeeze out the excess. Place it in the microwave for about 30 seconds. (Remembering to firstly remove the remains of last night's baked-on pizza – after all, you don't want a tomato, mozzarella and pineapple face-mask as well now do you?)

Take it out and place over your beard area leaving it on for a minute and letting the resulting steam open your pores. Take it off and apply some type of cream or gel to the beard (never use foam – this contains mostly air and doesn't lift the bristles enough to do a good job) and rub it in well. Leave for 30 seconds to make the little blighters sit up straighter than the front row at a Sugababes concert and ready to be lopped off quicker than Henry VIII's ex-wives. Take hold of your weapon of choice, either a single, double, triple or the recently introduced five-bladed monster from Gillette and start to shave in the following order:

Shaving in the direction of the hair growth, start from your sideburn then go diagonally across your cheek to your chin, all the time keeping the skin taut by pulling with your thumb. Continue across the chin and then down the neck, again working in the direction of the hair growth. Remember to rinse the blade regularly in clean hot water to remove the shaved hairs and lather.

Never shave against the direction of hair growth, as this may cause irritation (even worse than your old man banging on the toilet door demanding to be let in as he's desperate to use the loo) and possible ingrowing hairs.

Finally, shave your upper lip from the middle outwards, as these hairs tend to be the strongest and should be left till last to allow the lather to fully soften them. After you've finished, check for missed hairs then rinse your face in cool – but not freezing – water. Dry and then apply a moisturizing balm or moisturizer to stop the skin drying out. You should now have a smooth, nick-free skin.

If you choose to use either a cut throat (and they can you know) or a double edged safety razor instead of any of Mr Gillette's offerings, I recommend you use a cream applied with a good brush and possess a really steady hand. If you don't and are considering using one of these extremely effective but ultimately limb removing implements, may I suggest you first pay for a session with a qualified and experienced barber who will teach you the correct techniques. Although initially expensive will be money well spent.

A BODY TO DIE FOR

This is the part of your anatomy that usually enjoys the least exposure to a woman's gaze compared to the rest. However, in this section we're going to try to address this imbalance and get it in tip-top order for when that day finally arrives.

The way to guarantee a body a woman will want to run her hands over is much easier than you think. Like the face, it starts with the basics of showering or bathing at least twice daily. Use a body brush or sponge to loosen dead skin cells and make your skin tingle and shine. Should you have them, also remember to condition chest and pubic hair regularly too, as pubes with the consistency of barbed wire will guarantee that the only hand making that southerly journey will be your own.

If your penchant for chest hair matches the majority of this season's premiership stars, then my advice regarding hair removal is 'often is best'. As a male stripper I shaved not only my chest, but my whole body. On the odd occasion when I was unable to repeat the act daily due to a busy diary, I could guarantee that as soon as a willing punter started to rub in their handful of baby oil I was greeted with a shrill exclamation of "Ooh, you're all stubbly." An unshaven face against her skin is uncomfortable but the discomfort is multiplied ten fold after 20 minutes of horizontal bedroom athletics. For your sake and her skin, keep it smooth.

If shaving your body fills you with dread, then there are a number of depilatory (hair removal) creams on the market that will do the job for you.

After drying yourself off, moisturize all over using a good lotion containing aloe vera or cocoa butter. Trim those armpit hairs. You don't have to shave them off completely, but despite women often being suckers for cute furry mammals, won't take kindly to Chewbacca and his brother as sitting tenants in your underarm department.

The last step is to apply a deodorant to keep you fresh. Choose either a spray type or roll-on. Personally I prefer the ball type as it tends to last longer, keeps you drier and doesn't leave white marks on your best black shirt as though you've been leaning against wet paint. In addition, in today's world of global warming, loads of women just adore a man who shows some responsibility for the future of his planet.

You're now done – seems a shame to cover it all up with clothes – but that's the next chapter.

EXTREMITIES – MAKE THEM STAND OUT

Your face and hands are seen by others on a daily basis. Your feet less so, but it's still worth spending some time on them for when the socks come off and they slip between her Egyptian cotton sheets for some fun.

Let's start with the hands though. Along with our eyes, our hands are one of the most well used and expressive parts of our bodies. In body language they give out an endless supply of signals on how we feel and what we want. Therefore it's worth taking the time to make them look their best. They should, like the rest of your anatomy, be washed regularly and especially after visiting the toilet. Take special care to clean under your nails as well. If women feel that you can't be bothered to clean your nails, there's no imagining what they'll think about the rest of you and they won't even consider touching you to find out.

Trim and file your nails regularly, preferably straight after a shower or bath when the skin is soft, pushing back your cuticles gently with an orange stick wrapped in cotton wool. Contrary to what some macho guys think, doing this will not elevate you to the *Brokeback Mountain* school of cowboys. Ask yourself, do you really want to be responsible for making her back look like something out of *Nightmare on Elm Street*? I thought not, so start filing or get yourself a manicure. A good hand cream massaged in after filing will also keep them smooth and touchable.

Let's now travel downstairs to the opposite end of the body, the feet. In my opinion, feet are just ugly hands, shoved in socks most of the day. They are only paid any attention to when there's either a problem or you start running out of socks without holes. However, I am a strong believer that they deserve the same attention as hands, because you never know when the opportunity may arise to give them an airing and there are female foot fetishists around too you know.

Like hands, remember to wash your feet regularly in the shower or bath. Occasionally massage in some body scrub to exfoliate the little blighters and get rid of any build up of dead skin cells. After drying, remember to file the nails smooth as you don't want to be responsible for snagging her Laura Ashley sheets, now do you? Check for any lumps or extra toes growing and should you find anything, literally hotfoot it down to your local podiatrist to get them treated. Massage in some foot cream for good measure and they'll be happy to slip into whatever footwear and between anyone's duvet you choose.

Whether or not you're happy with the shape of your nose or not, one very common and unwelcome visitor to this body part will cause more damage to your chances of pulling faster than a porcupine in a condom factory – the dreaded dangling nasal hair. It is a mystery to all who reach a certain age, that the hair on your head diminishes whilst the strong, barb-like thatch that protrudes from our nasal cavities takes on the length and consistency of Tarzan's favourite form of jungle transport. It may sound mad, but it's almost like there's some invisible magnetic pull that almost sucks the hair down through your head to poke out through your nose. Perhaps if we stood on our heads it may reverse the situation. I think I've just invented a cure for baldness... Now where's that application form for *The Dragon's Den*?

The way to cut a nasal hair's marauding journey short is simple. A lot of people make the same fatal mistake of plucking these nasty buggers. Don't. If you do, not only will it make your eyes sting, but you will also cause an infection and you will end up looking like Rudolph (the reindeer, not Nureyev).

The answer is to get a sharp pair of nail scissors (make sure to wash them before and afterwards, especially if they are your mother's). Trim the hairs carefully back – taking great care not to cut yourself. Keep an eye on them too, as they have a nasty habit of creeping back up on you unannounced. Alternatively, if the thought of shoving a pair of sharp scissors up your nose fills you with dread, a lot of chemists sell small pocket clippers designed especially for this orifice so shell out some cash and buy one of these instead.

Regarding your trouser topiary, trim it occasionally into whatever style takes your fancy. (By the way, an upwards path shaved straight up makes your penis appear longer – a stripper's trick). Remember to condition it every couple of days when you shower. As for your most treasured extremity of all, apart from cleaning and taking as much exercise as possible (with a partner is better) you'll be pleased to know he's virtually maintenance free.

SMILE – THIS WON'T HURT A BIT

A beaming genuine smile coupled with direct eye contact or a wink is the strongest signal you can give to someone you're attracted to them. In practice this is all well and good if your teeth rival those of toothpaste ad gods Richard 'hamster' Hammond or Simon 'smug git' Cowell. However, should they be nearer to resembling Shane McGowan's pearly whites then it's lips tightly sealed until you have made that long overdue trip to the dentist for some painful and, dare I say, expensive work.

For those of us who find ourselves somewhere in between (and I'm one) here are a few basic rules guaranteed to transform your common-or-garden frog into a handsome prince.

Start with brushing twice a day – especially after eating – and finishing off with dental floss. However, remember to do it gently – you're not sawing through MDF. Make sure you visit your dentist at least every six months. By the way, a 'visit' means actually going in and sitting on the chair, not just popping in to say 'hello' to the tasty receptionist, picking up a new toothbrush and then leaving.

Apply a lip balm or Vaseline liberally in harsh winter weather to prevent chapping and to keep those lips kissable. A pocket breath freshener spray should always be kept handy too just in case a chance to chat with a tasty lady presents itself minutes after you've finished those three slices of garlic soaked bread from Pizza Hut. Remember to always check your smile in the mirror before leaving the house and again especially after eating. The remains of that salad lunch stuck between your teeth looks to others very much like you're a plant fetishit caught kissing a budding laburnum bush.

It's important too to practise your smile. I know it may sound a strange bit of advice, but you really don't know how you appear to others when you're smiling. You may be under the impression that your grin is one that portrays sophistication. However, in reality others may see you as one of the competitors off *Strictly Come Dancing* or alternatively an ideal candidate for the part of the Cheshire cat in the Hippodrome's annual

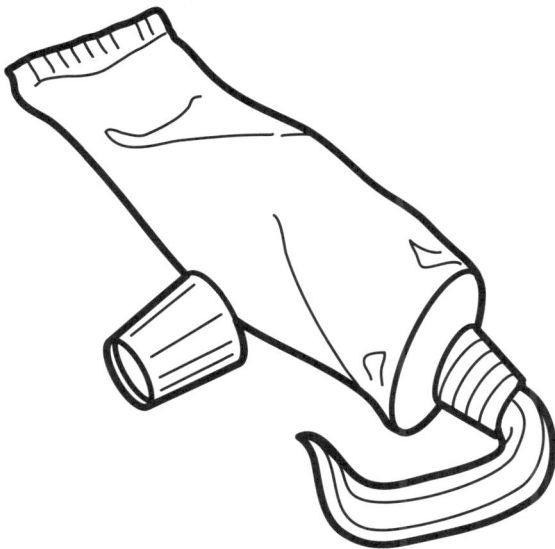

Dazzle, don't deter – keep some toothpaste handy for all emergencies

production of *Alice in Wonderland*. It pays to practise smiling because flashing just the right amount of enamel may get you noticed, but too much and she could be blinded.

I personally found out about the power of a smile when I was stripping. Women very often commented on how gorgeous my smile was – which was surprising really, as they had just seen me naked. Women, I ask you ...

SHE NOSE YOU KNOW

In this section I'm going to share with you, the lucky reader, the smells that have been scientifically proven to make women hornier than a Spanish bullfight. Contrary to what television and magazine advertising campaigns will have you believe, it's not Mr. Beckham's extremely expensive cologne. Nor is it a single pheromone, 'laboratory isolated' and advertised two for the price of one in the back pages of your Sunday paper.

It's so much more simple than that and you'll be pleased to know that all of the ingredients can be found quite easily and cheaply on display at your local 24 hour corner shop. According to scientists they are:

- **Toothpaste**
- **Baby powder**
- **Liquorice**
- **Cucumber**

I don't really understand it myself, but the above innocent-looking (apart from the cucumber that is) items mixed together are supposed to create a combination guaranteed to get women swooning.

Women have a much keener sense of smell than men. How we smell to them can have the effect of making them either drool like a dog tied up outside a butcher's shop or else have them reaching for the sick bag.

For those of you still not convinced by the above stated scientific formulae and rightly wary of walking around head to toe in white powder, overdosing on allsorts and sporting a large green vegetable in your

///RULES OF ATTRACTION//

Leave it one day before calling her. Any sooner and you'll appear desperate. Leave it longer and she may lose interest.

1

trousers, we will switch to what are the best fragrances available to buy in the shops.

Obviously, the actual smell you wear matters, but we will come onto that later. Firstly let's cover the biggest no-no as far as the male musk is concerned – overindulgence. Pouring it quicker than a lager shandy on a sunny day is not just wasteful as the stuff costs a bloody fortune, but will only serve to attract the local wasp population. The best bet is to get yourself a bottle with a spray nozzle instead.

The best way to use it effectively and economically is to spray it on your pulse points – your Adam's apple, the back of your neck and inside your wrists and elbows. Why not try my favourite way? Simply spray a blast into the air at head height and, remembering to close your eyes, simply walk through the mist to get a light coating all over. This way the bottle lasts longer and the smell is not too overpowering.

Now we come to which fragrance to choose. There are literally thousands of fragrances out there sitting on shop shelves almost hypnotically willing us to buy them with their bright packaging and expensive advertising. Selecting the one that's just right for you can be a real nightmare, but here are some tips that may help. When you're out looking to buy, never accept the sales assistant's kind offer to spray a tester on a card to take away as any fragrance smells completely different in this way to how it would on your person. Instead, ask her to spray some on the back of your hand.

Another helpful tip is to only choose two test sprays at a time. Spraying on any more will only confuse your sense of smell as it can easily mix them up and confuse the issue even more.

Let the tester fragrance stay on your hand for a couple of minutes and then smell it again. If it's still so strong it knocks your head off then it's not the one for you. However, if you can just about tell it's there, then decision made.

Alternatively, ask a female shopper what she thinks and use your body language and conversation skills to good effect and grab a date. Asking someone's opinion on a fragrance is a fantastic and non-threatening opening approach. Interestingly, this approach was used on myself by two girls a few weeks ago whilst I was out shopping. Two gorgeous young ladies approached me in the fragrance section of a leading department store and asked for my opinion on which fragrance one of the ladies should buy for her boyfriend. To cut a long story short, I discovered that the whole fragrance thing was just a ruse to get to speak to me. As a happily married man I was left with no choice but to refuse the ladies' offers.

Another common mistake made by a lot of guys when choosing fragrance is to concentrate on the well-known named and expensive brands, in the belief that all that fantastic packaging and advertising somehow make them superior. This is not the case and I can recount a personal true story to illustrate it. As a stripper I used to cover myself in aftershave prior to going on stage. Working four, five, six or seven nights a week this obviously became very expensive to maintain using my usual expensive brand. One day, whilst I was in a 'pound' shop picking up my monthly supply of baby oil, I spotted a bottle of aftershave called Bosun. Now as the shop's name suggests, all items were selling at a pound, so I bought a couple of bottles thinking that if it smelt as I

///**RULES OF ATTRACTION**//

Chat-up lines are rubbish. Don't use them. Women will tell you they only work when combined with copious amounts of alcohol.

thought it would do then even if I tipped it down the sink I hadn't wasted much money. However, I was to be proved totally wrong.

That night I wore some of this new brand sprayed onto the vest I wore on stage, which I then ripped down the centre and threw into the audience. The reaction from the women was amazing. It was like a scene from a *Natural World* programme, where a lion kills an antelope and the rest of the pride join in. The women tore the vest into strips in order to get a piece for themselves. They then sat through the rest of my performance with eyes glazed over like glue-sniffing teenagers. To prove it wasn't a one-off. I did the same thing for the following few nights and the effect was identical. Ladies were approaching me during the interval and at the end of the evening all asking what fragrance I was wearing. Suffice to say the next day I bought a case of bottles and, in addition to wearing it on stage, I even went on to sell them to the audience after the show at a huge profit for them to take home to their husbands and boyfriends.

This cheap aftershave, when mixed with my own natural scent, obviously suited me. Try this out for yourself. Don't always go for high cost and snob value, try out other cheaper and not so well known brands and like me, you may well strike it lucky.

CHAPTER FOUR:
DRESS TO IMPRESS

Done up like a dog's dinner

I can't see the point of me telling you all the good advice given in the previous chapters if you're going to throw it all away by going out looking for love without making at least the same effort in the way you dress.

We need only look at our cousins in the animal kingdom to discover that like them, dressing up in order to attract a mate is the order of the day. If it works for them it can certainly work for you too. Mother Nature certainly did not need an image consultant, so neither do you.

Women are not blind and, if you are going to increase your chances with them then it's time to examine what you currently wear. Attack that wardrobe and be prepared to donate and clothe someone who's not as well-off as you.

It's a known fact that ninety-three per cent of attraction is based on what we see and how people look. However, although being able to stand out from the crowd can often be referred to as an art it need not, as can often be thought, be expensive. A couple of well-chosen, well-made and classy items can go a long way to making you look good. As long as you let the mirror be your guide and not the assistants in the high street, then you're onto a winner.

In this chapter I am going to share with you some basic dressing tips. Should you decide to follow them will go a long way to making you look good without you really even having to try that hard. Do not worry if you do not grasp them all at once. All of us have been fashion victims sometime in our life (me included) so you are in esteemed company – do not worry.

First things first. It is time to have a look at what's lurking in your wardrobe at the moment. Take out everything and lay it on the bed or if there's too much then just put it on the floor, somewhere you can see exactly what's what. Now this is the point I need you to be really hard. Apart from seasonal coats and summer togs, take anything that hasn't been worn in the last six months and shove it in a black plastic bag. All this my friend, and there may well be a lot, is destined for the local charity shop as the grateful recipients will get more wear out of it than you have.

Carrying out this one small task will result in you feeling better about yourself in three ways. One, by getting rid of items connected with your negative past you're also ridding yourself of the same negative feelings attached to it.

Secondly, there is now loads of room to store all the new stuff you are going to go out and buy on your next trip up town. The stuff you do buy you will actually want to wear and will make you feel great about yourself. Thirdly, as mentioned earlier, that big bag of clobber you're going to offload will benefit someone who doesn't have the money, let alone the opportunity to buy gear like that – never mind how bad you feel it may look.

Your wardrobe is waiting to be filled so it is time to go over some simple golden rules to remember when out shopping for new stuff:

· **When choosing new items, think about what you've already got at home. You want your clothes to co-ordinate so, if shopping for jeans or trousers, wear the shoes and type of top you're going to be wearing with them. This way they'll look perfect together and it'll look like you've actually planned what you've bought. I've seen so many of my friends ignore this rule then find out that the jeans they got look they've had a divorce from their trainers and the jacket they wanted to wear with them was the wrong colour so plan ahead.**
· **Try not to buy just one item at a time. Instead, think like a woman and try and get yourself a whole outfit in one go. Take it from me, women are experts at this. What man can honestly hold up his hand and say he has never before in his life heard those immortal words: 'Now I've got those jeans I just must have some shoes to go with them. Oh, and a top.'**

Shopping this way means you'll spend a lot less time actually going shopping, more time wearing the stuff and you'll look ten times better for it. As you get more practiced, you'll also get to know what looks good on you. Remember what suits one person may look awful on another. By all means copy other people who look good, models in adverts or someone famous who dresses well, but remember this rule and try and find your own style and stick to it.

A word of caution, do not worry about keeping up with the latest fashion trends. They change frequently to deliberately fill designers' and store owner's pockets and empty yours. If you fall for it, you'll be spending more time with the bank manager instead of showing off to the ladies just how good you look.

If you don't have one already, then it's time to invest in that most important piece of furniture to grace your bachelor pad since the delivery of that La-Z-Boy leather armchair with built-in massager and fridge. It's not as expensive as the armchair and not as comfortable to sit on, but will quickly replace your dog as your best friend and won't chew up your new cross-train, ergonomic, slip-free-soled trainers either. It is simply a full-length mirror. A quick glance in it before leaving the house every day will let you see how others see you and avoid any ghastly fashion mistakes.

One minute's work with it means you can make any needed last-minute alterations before going out and hitting the town.

When choosing something to wear, it's also a good idea to think about a body part you may be particularly proud of (remember our opening self-confidence chapter?) If you have it then show it off.

///**RULES OF ATTRACTION**//

Ask simple, open questions that produce more than a 'yes' or 'no' response. Listen to her answers and store the personal information she provides for later use.

Remember though to be sensible. Mikey from *American Chopper*
is always seen in shorts whatever the weather, but ask yourself
if you've ever seen him with a woman except his mum? If you've
got good arms then wear something with short sleeves. If it's good
shoulders or chest then accentuate them both by wearing something
tight with horizontal strips for a great look.

When shopping, give shop assistants a wide berth (unless they're
gorgeous female ones, then they're fair game). They are generally
paid on commission and are well-trained to say you look gorgeous in
whatever you try on. They will happily and without guilt divest your
wallet of its hard-earned cash so steer well clear.

One type of shop assistant you can take advantage of (not that
way) is the personal shoppers found in all the major department
and large clothing chain stores. Call up in advance and make an
appointment to see one. After chatting with you for a few minutes
to find out your measurements and a little about the style you want
to achieve, they'll scoot off round the store leaving you to enjoy a
sit down and a complimentary coffee. Half an hour later they'll be
back with armfuls of great gear for you to try on. It doesn't cost you
anything, there's no obligation to buy and it cuts down on both your
leg and guess work.

I always avail myself of this service when I'm in a big city as it's so
relaxing to have someone do all the hard work for you.

In this next section we are going to look at a few tips on colour
and style options to suit different body types – first those suitable
for the slimmer man and then for those who Mother Nature
bestowed with a little more muscle and brawn. Find out what section
you belong to, take notes and next time you're out in the high street
you'll get exactly what 'suits you, sir'.

SKINNY GUYS

· **Choose horizontal stripes and paler colours to give the illusion of breadth**

· **When buying suits, choose looser cut styles avoiding narrow-cut jackets as they only serve to accentuate your slim frame. Choose a grey background with either large checks or broad stripes to add the illusion of breadth to your physique. Horizontal or diagonal stripes on your tie will also add to that illusion.**

· **Wear pale trousers to add bulk to your legs, also making sure they are not too slim fitting or too baggy as both can draw attention to your skinny legs**

· **Go for bold squares or broad stripes when choosing shirts and add a plain tie or one with horizontal stripes.**

· **Never team up a patterned shirt with a patterned tie – you'll just look a mess.**

· **When shopping for jeans, avoid dark shades and, again, don't go too baggy or too tight.**

· **T-shirts and casual tops should be pale in colour and not too baggy. Skin-tight is a definite no-no.**

SHORT AND STOCKY TYPES

- **Wearing darker colours with pale vertical stripes will make you appear taller and leaner.**
- **Avoid double-breasted suits and go for a soft-cut single-breasted style, making sure the jacket is long enough to cover your bum – otherwise it will look even bigger.**
- **Choose dark trousers, as they will minimize your bum, and also avoid pleated fronts, as they can make your waist appear larger than it actually is.**
- **Make sure your shirt is also dark, but not as dark as your suit, and choose a tie with fine vertical stripes to give the impression of length to your body.**
- **When choosing jeans, make sure the denim is dark and in a fitted style – baggy jeans only increase the bulk of your legs.**
- **Avoid polo neck tops, and instead opt for v-neck styles, again in dark colours, to make your neck appear longer.**

There are thousands of tips and hints on how to wear clothes and what looks good with what, but I'm going to have to leave you wanting more. This is just the tip of the iceberg, so use the information above as a starting point and begin experimenting with different styles, fabrics and colours till you get a look that is just you. You never know, my next book might just be dedicated to this subject alone!

Personally I have found the best way to choose clothes to suit is to look around and see what everyone else is wearing. Models in adverts on television and in the media in general are not exactly 'normal'. In my opinion they should never be considered as role models for the average man in the street. Let's face it, they are selected because they are 25, stand 8 foot tall in their stockinged feet, are tanned with a six-pack, have pecs like Action Man and everything they wear looks great on them. Therefore, it stands to reason then that a 5' ginger 49-year-old with a beer belly covering both his belt and a clear view of his penis will just look ridiculous in whatever label is flavour of the month today.

What I do when I'm out is look around to see what everyone else is wearing. If I see a guy my height and build and he looks good in his gear, then I make a mental note of what he's wearing and go out and copy him. After all, imitation is the sincerest form of flattery so everyone's happy. I sometimes take it further and will even ask where he got the particular item.

One specific time this tactic worked well was a few years ago when I was shopping for new glasses and try as I might I just couldn't decide on the right pair. Sitting having a coffee in Starbucks and annoyed because I was getting nowhere, I happened to spot a guy wearing a really trendy pair of frames that suited him to a tee. He was the same build, like me shaved his head and looked really cool. I literally ran out of the shop, leaving my coffee, and stopped and politely asked him where he had bought them. Not only did he tell me, he actually took them off, gave me the manufacturer, frame number, where he had bought them and how much he had paid. What a top bloke.

Now I am certainly not advocating you run up and down the street 24/7 accosting strange blokes in the street otherwise you may find yourself in a whole spot of bother. However, on the odd occasion it does work – try it yourself sometime. Follow these basic rules and that suit you wear to the club one night may just end up with her wearing the best outfit you could have hoped for: her birthday suit.

Happy shopping.

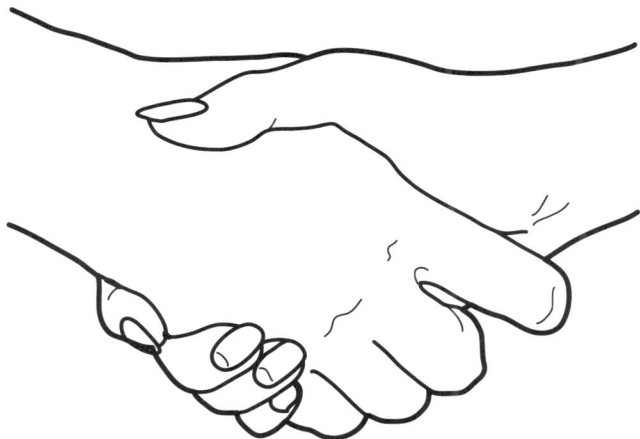

A manly sign – but do you know all hers?

CHAPTER FIVE:
GROUNDWORK

The A to Z of flirting...

FIND YOUR WAY OUT OF THE MAZE

Now we have reached the real nitty gritty section of this book. The preceding chapters are all important, but here is the section I think you'll admit to really have been waiting for. In this section I'm going to lay bare all the techniques you are ever going to need to know to really make a killing when out on the pull. We're going to cover how to tell if someone's really interested or just being friendly, how to approach her, what to say and how to up the level to raise the stakes and take home first prize.

However, before we go diving headlong into minute detail about actually how to attract a woman, the first thing to take into consideration is that there are more than the most obvious places like nightclubs and pubs where women congregate. The truth of the matter is that women are all around you 24/7 and are all legitimate targets to try out the techniques I'm about to teach you.

Likely candidates can be found where you work, standing next to you on the bus or tube, working in shops, taking their dogs for a walk in the park or in the gym. In fact, everywhere you turn there are women around. Later on we are going to cover how to focus and concentrate your techniques in specific locations, however the basics are the same and should be followed and can adapted for many different situations.

A couple of years ago a friend of mine was extremely jealous of my success with the ladies. He used to continually bend my ear and complain about his own barren love life. To try and get to the bottom of why he wasn't having any luck I asked him where he went to meet women. To say I was gobsmacked by his reply is an understatement! It transpired

///**RULES OF ATTRACTION**//

Mirror her positive body language signals but wait 30 seconds otherwise she'll think you're Pinocchio.

that apart from work and a quick pint in his local on a Saturday night, the guy never left the house.To think he wondered why he wasn't meeting anyone! Now I'm not saying anyone who is reading this is as bad as he was, but I'm sure you can see the point I'm making. To give yourself any chance of success you have to be out there. Like fishing, you need to cast your net wide and over new and uncharted waters.

Another important thing you need to learn before you have any hope of getting past first base is the fundamental (we want fun and women can go mental) difference between what is 'friendly' and what is 'flirting'. Unfortunately most men are just hopeless at separating the two. A woman on the other hand, is easily able to distinguish between them. Thid means the onus is on you to carry out your research and bridge the knowledge gap on those tell tale signs between her being just plain friendly and being interested – as they do exist, I promise.

The answer, quite simply is something called body language. Body language is the silent and almost subliminal way we communicate with each other, the majority of the time without us even realizing it. Every waking hour, whatever we are doing, our body language is signalling to people how we feel and what we are thinking. As I mentioned earlier in the grooming section, only 7 per cent of communication is actually verbal. This equates to 93 per cent of stuff that is almost as alien to a man as having to order his San Miguel in the native tongue of the country in which he is taking his holiday.

Sure, most of us recognize a small number of common signals – such as the handshake we use daily translating as openness and trust. Another favourite is the arms folded, signifying a barrier that says 'don't come too close' – although some of us do tend to ignore that one, depending on who we're talking to. Remember last Friday and the blonde you were grilling for four-and-a-half hours in the pub? She was trying to say 'I'm cold, tired and bored out of my head and will you please stop looking at my chest' but still you carried on! All of us recognize these and other obvious signs. However, there are hundreds of subtle signs used between males and females in the mating game that require further explanation.

I want you to concentrate on what I'm now going to tell you, because I'm going to show you step by step the techniques I have personally used to great success and believe me they really do work. For this example we'll use the scenario of the pub or club – but remember, as I said earlier, these techniques can be used to great effect anywhere. Just tailor them to suit your particular situation and you're onto a winner.

Although you should now be brimming with confidence after following the PSP techniques mentioned in an earlier chapter, I'm just going to cover a couple of quick on the spot confidence 'fix its' just in case your steely nerve starts to desert you.

The first thing to do is breathe. I know this sounds obvious, but look at any nervous or shy person and the overwhelming thing you notice they do is hold their breath. By taking a deep breath before speaking you steady yourself, giving yourself a valuable second or two to think about what it is you're going to say. It also lowers your voice slightly so you sound sexy and not like old squeaky King of the Jungle – Joe Pasquale.

Secondly, make sure you stand straight and at least look like a confident person. Remember the exercise we covered in the chapter on sex appeal? Standing straight, shoulders back and head high gives everyone the message that you're happy with the way you look and it's a green light for them to approach.

So let's start out with you arriving at the club. As you enter the door, frame yourself in the doorway for a second or two, giving every person, but especially the women time to turn, look and check you out, and in turn, you them.

As you enter, don't forget to smile. Select someone who's standing a little towards the centre of the room, fix your gaze on them and smile. Don't worry if they don't return your smile. With so many people in the room, everyone will automatically think you're looking at someone else anyway so there's no real chance of a negative reaction.

If there's a focal point in the room, such as a bar, then get yourself over to it, remembering to walk through the centre of the room first. Doing this emphasises to everyone your confidence. As you walk, be aware of who

///**RULES OF ATTRACTION**//

When you call her – at least one day after getting her number – do not get phased if you only get her voice mail. Leave a simple name including your name, how you enjoyed meeting her and your number.

1

is in the room and where they're standing in readiness for later. Position yourself against the bar so you've a good view of the rest of the room. Start to look around very slowly, checking out the talent and making a mental note of where the most attractive women are standing, what they're wearing, who they're with and if they're looking in your direction.

Whilst standing, make sure your body is saying what you really want it to say. Turn your body towards the crowd and let your arms hang relaxed. Alternatively, place one hand in your pocket but let your thumb poke out. Thumbs showing in body language terms denote an air of confidence and pointing downwards towards your genitals doubles the message you're trying to project. Start to shift your weight onto one leg as this too is a very powerful position and also makes you look less stiff and awkward.

Remember, it takes a woman less than ten seconds or so to form a lasting opinion of you, so make sure your first impressions really do count and don't blow it before you've even started.

If any of the women in the room do catch your eye, then here's what to do to start the ball rolling. Start by meeting her gaze for about ten seconds and then look around the room again slowly as if you're looking for someone else before returning your gaze back to her. If she looks away and then returns to look at you, then you're over the first hurdle as it's obvious she's interested.

By looking around the room again after the initial eye contact and then returning your gaze to hers, you're delivering a very powerful message to her subconscious telling her that out of all the women in the room it's her that you find the most attractive.

Doing this also gives you valuable time to again check out the rest of the talent in the room, just in case things don't go smoothly with your intended target. Now repeat the previous action by looking down this time then again returning your gaze to meet hers. If she's still looking, she'll be intrigued and just willing you to come over.

However, one thing you must never do while looking at her, is stare. By staring you'll only serve to unnerve her. You will begin to resemble Hannibal Lechter and the chances will be high that she'll be off the menu tonight, a nice glass chianti or not. As you're looking, start to blink a little more regularly than normal. Blinking tells people that either we fancy them or we've got something in our eye and we need help. As you increase the speed of your blinking, make a note if she does the same and matches your speed. If she does then things are looking good.

Again, remember to smile, but make sure it's natural as there's nothing more off-putting to a woman than a man who wears a grin so forced it looks like he's been undergoing a rather painful session of colonic irrigation. Just relax and be yourself. This is where a lot of men make the same old mistake. They get so hung up on trying hard to impress a woman that they try too hard and completely forget who they really are. While she's looking at you, it is time to bring into play a very powerful weapon from your arsenal (and I don't care if you support United). While she's still looking over, lightly pat or scratch a piece of your anatomy that you feel confident with. It could be your biceps, your chest or even that ultra-trendy (for the next three days, anyway) hairstyle you've just paid half a month's salary for. In this situation I used to lightly touch my biceps or rub my hand over my shaved head, but it really doesn't matter where you rub (though your groin is obviously out of bounds (well until later hopefully anyway).

Touch or lightly scratch it while still maintaining eye contact, as this sends a powerful message to her subconscious reinforcing your

///**RULES OF ATTRACTION**//

Do not be tempted to tell her lies about what you do to earn your living. It just is not worth it. There is more chance of you succeeding by being honest.

attractiveness and selling yourself to her further. To up the ante, try giving her a little wink whilst smiling and carrying out your gesture as all three are like a thunderbolt and will knock her out. Check out her body language continually, paying her feet special attention. If they're pointing in your direction slightly apart, then it's the green light. The same applies if she's sitting. Look out for her crossing her legs at the thighs, wrapping one foot around the other ankle or letting her sandal or shoe dangle off the end of her toes. These poses all tell you that she's interested so it's time to make your move.

If she's in the room on her own, then leave it a minute of two before approaching to see if she's waiting for someone else to join her. If she is and it's another female, then it's safe to make your move. However, continue to act with caution, as her wrestler boyfriend might well be just the gents and will be hitting you with a fist the size of a small car the minute you step out of line.

If she is with a friend, you may well be better off taking a mate for support. Why's that you ask? Firstly, you'll need to split them up and women can be harder to separate than a couple of rutting Rottweilers. Secondly, having to divide your time between both of them makes it even more difficult to pull, as you cannot concentrate your efforts on the one you really want.

Have you ever noticed that you very rarely see two attractive women together out on the town? I have a theory about that, and although it sounds sexist, that couldn't be further from my mind. I think the attractive one out of the two goes out with her plainer friend simply to make her appear even better in comparison. Similarly, the plain friend goes out with the attractive one to take advantage of all the attention her mate gets from the guys and pick up any strays that are cast aside. This ploy can be used to your advantage, as your mate can distract the ugly sister while you give Cinders your undivided attention. If he's a real mate he won't mind either.

So it's now time to make your approach. If at this crucial stage your nerve takes a wobble here's a quick fix-it – just change the way you think about her. Instead of putting pressure on yourself by thinking 'will she like me'? Flip the whole concept on it's head and change the question you're asking to 'I wonder if I'll like her'? Doing this simple thing takes the pressure off and you're more likely to appear normal, not nervous. Smile at her again and make your way over. Women are more receptive to approaches made directly from the front and when you look at this it's really quite understandable. It all harks back to Neanderthal times when if something came upon you from the side or the back it generally wanted to eat you so as you approach. Check to see if her stance alters. If she moves from how she's been standing and squares up to you then she's looking forward to your approach.

As you approach, remember to try and position yourself at her left hand side if possible. It's a scientifically proven fact that information absorbed through a woman's left ear is more likely to be retained, as that side of the brain is responsible for processing emotional information. Men on the other hand, use 99 per cent of their brains to store information on booze, pornography and football and the remaining one per cent to remember emotional stuff and what a woman tells them! When you finally get to her it's now time to put your money where your mouth is and actually start speaking. If you forget everything else written in this book, please just take with you this one golden rule – chat-up lines simply do not work. There are books galore on the market promoting this type of rubbish information. Try as hard as you might, you won't find any in here and that's a promise. The correct way to success is a lot simpler and shorter. After all, you're only trying to break the ice, not sink the whole ship!

I find it unbelievable that in this day and age so many guys, are still put off from approaching women as they are under the impression that the first thing to come out of their mouth should be either clever, witty, charming, or a combination of all three. This is simply not the case. Obviously your initial introduction counts, but it's what you follow it up with that really matters. To start, the best thing to can do is introduce yourself by name and then ask an open question that's relevant to the situation and not too challenging.

An example of a good opening introduction for use in a club would be "Hi I'm Clive (obviously use your own name here), do you know why it is so busy here tonight?" or "What's the music like in here, it's my first time?" Keep it simple. The more ordinary and less obvious the better. try something that invites more of an answer than a simple "yes" or "no".

Using something simple and non-threatening means you've broken the tip of the iceberg. Now it is time to start chipping away at the polar ice cap underneath it bit by bit. Here's how it's done. Once you've opened the conversation, shut up and let her do the talking. After all, when God made man he gave him two ears and just one mouth. Use them in that proportion. Allow her the comfort of letting her go on and on about whatever she likes for as long as she likes completely uninterrupted. While she's doing this – it may take a while – I want you to take note of what she's saying, maintain eye contact at all times and nod in agreement, making positive noises when required or when she comes up for air. You could well be waiting a long time, but it'll be to your advantage.

While she's talking, stand facing her, keep your body language open and keep on smiling. We are all attracted to people who appear to like us so genuinely look as though you're enjoying yourself and in turn they'll enjoy talking to you more. As time goes on, they will become more relaxed and open up. At no point be tempted to interrupt and start banging on about yourself, how the Arsenal played a blinder on Saturday or start describing your entire extensive *Star Trek* memorabilia collection. It's a mistake so many men have made in the past and have paid dearly for. My own brother experienced this (the *Star Trek* example) one night at dinner on a first date. It remained a first date as at some point in the evening she went to the ladies' and yes, you've guessed it, she never came back. Your only responsibility for the moment is to watch and listen, as you will need to store the vital information she's sharing with you to fall back on later.

While she's talking, start to use your eyes to flirt and use what we call in the business as 'The Flirting Triangle'. The way we look at people's faces depends on how we feel about them. When talking to strangers and in formal business situations, our eyes trace the shape of an upside down triangle from both eyes down to a point across the bridge of the nose. This widens when we're talking to people we know well as the lower point of the triangle drops slightly to include the rest of the nose and the mouth and, when we really fancy someone, this point drops even further to include the breasts and occasionally the genitals. Now on no account am I advocating staring at her cleavage the whole evening. However, as the evening progresses and you both feel more relaxed, you should start to see eye contact between you becoming more friendly and open. This is where you can start to widen the area of your triangle, lingering on the mouth and making furtive little glances to the more interesting bits down south. See if she copies what your doing and also look to see if you recognize any other encouraging body language signals she's displaying that'll give the game away as to how she's feeling. Here are a just a few to commit to memory, although as I've mentioned previously there are loads more:

- **She looks at you and plays with her hair. By doing this she's subconsciously saying to you 'Look at me.'**
- **She's looking at your mouth lots. If she's copying your flirting triangle but is concentrating on your mouth then the more interested she's becoming. Raise the stakes even higher by suddenly licking your lips and look to see her temperature soar.**
- **She sits on the edge of her seat during the conversation trying to be as close as possible to you.**
- **When you offer her a drink, instead of wine she chooses something she can swig sexily straight from the bottle. If she then carresses the bottle in a rhythmical motion it may sound cliche'd but you're onto a winner as she's using the bottle to mimic just what she would like to do with you.**
- **She's still talking to you ten minutes after you bought her that first drink. If she wasn't interested she'd have been long gone. Test it out further by saying you have to pop out for a minute and she if she's waiting when you get back.**

- She massages her neck. Chances are if she does this she's not suffering from whiplash but for sure the Miss Whiplash in her is subtly pushing her breasts forward and wafting natural pheromones in your direction.
- During the conversation she says something like 'Your girlfriend would love that', which is a typical female fishing ploy to discover if you already have a lady in your life so remember to respond accordingly.
- She spends more than three minutes in the toilets (which is plenty for her to carry out her ablutions), so she must be making an effort just for you.
- She starts to fidget with her clothes. She may start to undo buttons or even remove layers. Unless the central heating's on full, you're the cause and it won't be long until she'll be repeating herself somewhere a little more private for both of you.
- She sits and flashes her inner thigh and touches her arms and legs. If she couples this with leaning towards you then like Jesse James of old, you're a wanted man.
- She's nibbling on the end of her straw or the arm of her glasses – this takes her back to a secure childhood feeling, like breastfeeding.

One other simple way to tell if she's becoming keen on you is to notice if she copies something that you do. This is a powerful technique called 'mirroring', one of the most sincerest forms of flattery and a sure fire sign that she's interested. We tend to mimic people we are interested in so test it for yourself while talking to her. Tilt your head slightly to one side or pick up your glass and take a drink, looking to see if she follows suit. If she does, then it tells you that things are rolling along nicely. Leave it a couple of minutes and try again. If she doesn't follow suit immediately, don't worry. Simply take the lead and copy something she does. Remember to leave a delay of between 30–40 seconds as, if you're too quick in copying she'll either think you're taking the mickey or have you down as Pinocchio the puppet. Mirroring doesn't solely have to be a physical copying either.

Another good way to mirror her is to use what she says and how she says it. Try repeating key words and the speed and tone of her voice. It has as powerful an effect as does physical gesturing.

On the other hand, should she gabbles on, hands folded tighter than an origami master's, does the exact opposite of every thing you do and disappears to 'Noah's' (the place where women always go two by two) returning after what seems an eternity looking no different, then it is obvious she's none too fussed about you. She is probably only chatting because she is feeling lonely as her boyfriend's out of town or she wants a free drink. While chatting start to ask probing questions. These should take the form of open questions that invite the listener to part with valuable information for you to use to your advantage at a later date. At this stage such questions should always appear innocent, friendly and along such lines as what her job is and what sort of things she does in her spare time.

As she's baring her life to you, now's the time to start connecting with her subconscious and putting her under your spell. One powerful way to do this is when she's sharing something she's really passionate about – like a film she's seen recently, a sport she really enjoys doing or a foreign holiday on the horizon – nod in agreement whilst maintaining eye contact and tell her that you feel exactly the same way as she does about it. By agreeing with her on something personal and appearing to be on her wavelength she'll automatically start warming to you more. This will make it easier to explore her mind – and her body at a later date.

A great true story of how this technique worked to my advantage starts when I was performing in a little town called Usk a few years back. Following the show I found myself in the bar with a fellow performer and a couple of very attractive girls. The girl my friend was talking to was all over him like the proverbial rash. However, the one I'd set my sights on, a tall blonde with an amazing figure, was unfortunately doing a very good impression of David Blaine in his block of ice stunt and I couldn't get near her. I tried everything I could think of but she wouldn't entertain me, due to the fact I found out later that I was a stripper. In her eyes, strippers were players, with no scruples combined with sordid reputations (as if!) My frustration was compounded by my friend's increasing success, culminating with his girl sitting on his lap and taking her top off. The Ice Queen sat next to me unimpressed by this debauchery. As the floor show got even steamier, her disgust just grew and grew. In desperation I decided to completely change my approach and so just sat and listened as she complained, nodding in agreement and also joining in verbally berating my friend for his disgusting display and his sexist attitude towards women. (He forgave me the next day for this). This continued until I seized my chance and I announced that I could watch the filthy exhibition no more, intended to leave and asked if the now melting Ice Queen wanted to come with me? She agreed, we were now soul mates and 'enjoyed' each others company through to the next morning. When talking to my friend over a well-deserved breakfast, he spluttered his amazement that I had managed to get anywhere at all considering the girl's initial reluctance. He begrudgingly admitted that on retiring, his fun had been curtailed by his partner passing out on the bed due to the amount of alcohol she had imbibed.

At this point let me warn you that when agreeing with her about the subject she's raving on about, never, ever lie. Like I mentioned earlier, when trying to impress the ladies, men find it impossible to be themselves. Whilst I know it's tempting to say that, like her, you've visited the sun-kissed isles of the Caymans, when in fact the closest you've been is Cleethorpes, it just isn't worth it. If you're a mechanic, then tell her. There is more chance of you succeeding by being honest with her than if you lie and say you're a professional footballer (and I have heard it said) or something equally ludicrous.

///**RULES OF ATTRACTION**//

When you frame yourself when entering a room, use the opportunity to look around as if you are searching for someone. While doing this, make a mental note of where the attractive women are.

F

While she's talking about the things she's passionate about, she'll be getting more excited – and therefore in a more receptive – frame of mind. Remember what was said in the chapter on PSP? This is when you make your move.. At this stage it's now time to bring into play a very powerful, and almost hypnotic technique taught to me by a friend who worked as a male escort for many years. I tried it on many occasions myself – and to very good effect, I can assure you. This is how it works. When she is at the height of her excitement, talking about her favourite subject, I want you to make a gesture. It need only be something very simple, innocent to anyone else in the room, but it'll turn out to be very powerful and significant to her. Adjust your watchstrap (but don't actually look at your watch or she'll think you're bored), loosen your shirt collar, or do something similarly innocuous. While carrying out this 'gesture', concentrate on maintaining eye contact with her. Carrying out these actions in tandem and, combined with her excited state of mind, prints your gesture into her subconscious automatically relating it to the pleasure she's been experiencing. If the conversation starts to flag at any time or you simply want to bring her back to her excited state, just repeat the gesture while again maintaining eye contact and it will work.

We have covered what to say and when to say it, but as yet not actually how to say it (there are many different ways, I can tell you). Ideally, as mentioned in the paragraph on mirroring, you should try and match her speed and tone of voice so you bond quicker. If she's an excitable sort then you too should raise your voice and speed up to match hers. Similarly, if she talks really slowly and deliberately, then you should respond in a slightly exaggerated manner in order that she has to lean in and concentrate on what you're saying. This is also an ideal time to use the information you extracted from speaking to her earlier. As the conversation continues, drop in key words, phrases and pieces of information she mentioned to you earlier, ones she'll think you've forgotten. Adding her name in occasionally also works wonders as it's the single sound we all react to the quickest. The fact that you actually listened and took note of what she said will impress her no end.

To take your conversation (and her) to the next level. I'm now going to introduce a very powerful conversational technique called 'phonetic ambiguity'. This is when common and innocent sounding words transform themselves to convey a deep hidden sexual meaning to those who hear them when used together as part of a sentence, a phrase or when special emphasis is placed on them. Phonetic ambiguity is designed to further act on the recipient's subconscious and open her up to the person delivering the lines. Make sure that the words and phrases used are relevant to the topic of conversation and that you don't emphasize the words too strongly as that'll just sound odd. Below are some examples of one's I've used myself and using the same principles it should be easy for you to think up others for yourself. In the examples below, the important words to be linked or emphasized are highlighted to help you see what I am getting at and should be used as a guide:

Examples:

· I bet you felt really **excited** standing at the top of the Eiffel Tower.
· I saw a **wonderful** sight the other day while out driving.
· You make **hard** work sound so easy.
· I'll be **coming** to that stage myself too, soon.
· I got caught in a downpour yesterday and was **dripping wet**.
· In you I think I've found someone who **feels** the same way.
· **I want you** to know I'm with you all the way.
· It's interesting to know how you feel **deep inside**.
· I bet you **feel on top** of the world when you're doing that.

I can imagine that when you first read the above examples you thought they sounded a little corny. Remember though, they are not being used in isolation like they appear on the page. Placing them into the context of a relevant topic of conversation coupled with positive body language signals and mirroring techniques will have the desired effect. She will soon be eating out of your lap. It's now time to ask her out.

CHAPTER SIX:
SEAL THE DEAL

What's the worst that can happen?

All that hard work has finally paid off and she's succumbed to your silver-tongued charm. Now is the time to move in for the kill and ask the lady for her number suggesting you meet up again to continue the conversation.

When dealing with the fairer sex, one very important point to remember is that women absolutely adore a man who appears in control. What other reason could there be for women with bodies like sirens to willingly get together with ugly politicians, dwarf-like magicians or a bloke who spends his waking hours with his hand up a three-foot green duck's bottom?

Ask for her number and make sure you write it down. I don't care if you're a fully paid up member of Mensa, never, ever commit it to memory, as anything could happen. Once you've lost it, all your hard work has been for nothing. While we're at it, never enter it into your mobile while she reads it out. She is bound to spy all the numbers of the other girls you've been trying to pull along with the number of that late-night sauna in the town, the one you swear you'll never call but never get rid of either.

The best way to impress her and remember it is to write it down on something important you're guaranteed not to lose. In this day and age, only Claims R Us accident solicitors carry a pen so ask the barman if you can borrow one. You will not need to ask for paper as I'm going to show you a clever trick I've used before and one I'm sure you'll like.

Take out a paper note from your wallet and write her number on it (or get her to do it). Read it back to her to make sure you haven't made any mistakes or if she is a doctor that you can understand her spidery handwriting.

She'll be impressed by you doing this as it'll appear to her that her number is doubly important to you. The higher the value of the note, the more important in your eyes she'll consider herself to be. A couple of words of warning when trying this though. Don't make too flash a gesture when taking out the note. Make it appear it's the only way to record her number. If she offers paper, then simply take it – there will be plenty of time to interest her later. Similarly, if you've spent up that evening and

The more expensive the note, the more she'll feel valued

only have a pocketful of coins don't try and scratch it on one – it won't work and she'll be well upset that she's only worth this little. If coins are all you have left after buying her 18 JDs, borrow a note off a mate or ask the barman for some paper as well as a pen.

Also, if you use a note, remember not to spend it at the kebab house on the way home or the only number you'll be calling will start with 0898 and will cost you a damn sight more than a twenty.

Another trick you can use to impress her using the note with her number on it (and for it to be successful, it should really be as big a bill as possible – you'll see why) is to put it in your back pocket and then tell her you can magic it into the bar till just by concentrating on it.

She'll be intrigued and obviously say that it's impossible or that you're drunk, but here's how it's done. Firstly, make sure the place is crowded and you have a friend who's already set up to help standing behind you.

Tell the girl that the trick requires complete concentration and ask her to focus her attention on the till, repeating that she needs to keep looking at it otherwise the trick won't work. At the same time do the same (mirroring again), as if willing the note to travel there by some sort of ESP. While you're doing this and the lady's attention is distracted, your mate takes the note out of your back pocket and slips round to the opposite side of the bar, buying a drink and ensuring the note gets into the till. (Make sure he's a good and honest mate first otherwise you may just see him slip out of the door with your twenty, her number and your credibility)

When he returns, ask the barman to look in the till to see if the note with her number on is there. If everything's gone as planned it will be, and she'll be impressed.

If, when you ask, she gives you her mobile number, give yourself 6/10. Her home number gets you a 9. However, anything that starts with 0898 gets you a big fat 0 as it's going to be a long-distance and very expensive relationship. If she refuses to give her number out but asks for yours instead, she's hedging her bets and isn't really sure of you (or is married or tied herself). Anyway, give it to her as you may still be in with a chance – just don't take it as an automatic rebuff. The very fact she asks for yours in the first place means she's interested, but wants to be the one in complete control. That's fair enough, it's still a positive result as you never know, you may just have impressed her enough to actually get her to make that call later. The other reason for doing this is that she may think you're married or shacked up with someone, so she wants to call you first to see if someone else answers. Women are crafty pieces of work you know.

After taking her number, tell her you'll call and actually mean what you say. If you've only been having some fun with her then don't push it and ask. If you are serious and do take it and then change your mind later then don't ignore her or chuck her number away. Do the decent thing and call or text to let her know. Be honest. Women are resilient creatures and can stand being let down if the bloke's honest, but don't like liars. And also remember that women talk to each other (what else do you think they do in the toilets for half an hour). Word spreads and your name could well be mud (or worse) the next time you step foot in your local club.

The next thing to consider is the timing of your call. This is crucial. Never call the same day, or even the next. By making her wait a little, in her mind you're taking control of the situation, building up her anticipation of your next meeting and this is something she likes. Call any sooner and she'll have you down as desperate. Adhering to this rule is most important.

The most effective time to call is two days after your first meeting. Also try to call when you know for sure she'll be alone. Never call her during work hours unless she tells you it's OK as she won't be in a good position to talk and may even get into trouble. If she doesn't answer when you call and you get her voice mail – don't hang up. Instead, leave a message.

///**RULES OF ATTRACTION**//

Smile. The best signal there is.

One girl I met admitted to me later on in the relationship that she didn't answer my first call deliberately as she thought my voice was so sexy she wanted it on tape. I could not believe it but that's women for you.

Don't witter on when leaving your message. Instead, keep it brief. Say who you are as after all, you haven't a clue how many blokes she gave her number to the other night (at least one other if that 'twenty in the till' trick went wrong!) Say you really enjoyed meeting her then and ask her to call you, leaving her your number and that's it. After all, you've made the first move, kept to your agreement and the ball's now well and truly in her court. Never make the mistake of ringing when you've had a few beers to steady your nerves, all slurring your words down the phone. Do this and you are guaranteed to get your number quickly and effortlessly erased from her phonebook and you from her memory.

If she is in when you call and answers, firstly listen to the tone of her voice when she realises it's you. Judge if she still sounds interested. She may have been a little drunk when giving out her number and be married and now have a guilt complex as wide as the tattoos across her hubby's back, so beware.

If she says 'Sorry, no-one lives here of that name', and you know for certain it's her, then she's obviously had time to think and has changed her mind. Similarly, if she slams the receiver down before you've finished stating your whole name then it may be painful to admit that you have been dumped but resist the temptation to re-dial and give her a mouthful. Discretion is the better part of valour. Be a man and take it squarely on the chin.

For the following example, though, we'll dwell no longer on the negative, but on the positive. You rang, she answered, she's pleased

---

///**RULES OF ATTRACTION**//

Is she blinking? One way of knowing whether she is interested is to see if her rate of blinking increases when looking at you.

to hear it's you and after a huge sigh of relief it's now time to fix the first date.

Start by asking her what she's been up to since you last met, remembering again to sound interested and use the same techniques where you repeat her name occasionally and mirror what she says. Having a conversation on the phone with someone has both it's advantages and disadvantages. One the plus side, she can't see that your hair's a mess and you haven't shaved, but the major disadvantage is that body language is useless, so to get the message across you must emphasize your voice even more.

Again, litter your conversation with open questions and after a while offer to take her out somewhere you know she will like (you will already know this if you did your homework when you first met her ...) However, also have an alternative back-up day and venue available just in case she cannot make the first.

If she gives you a can't-make-it-that-day excuse or similar, don't get angry and start sounding uptight or despondent. She's either too polite to tell you she's changed her mind or is fishing to see how much chasing you'll do before you give up. Try one more time and, if her diary's fuller than Bridget Jones', tell her again that you enjoyed meeting her, to take care and then do her dirty work for her and bow out gracefully. If everything's gone swimmingly and you've agreed a time, date and place to meet then again, as you did with her number, write it all down. The last thing you want to do is ring her back later because you've forgotten.

Read on and discover more ways to help yourself score.

CHAPTER SEVEN:
PULLING TOOLS

30

Who's a DIY man?

In the previous chapter on 'groundwork', I emphasised the importance of acting naturally and being yourself when in conversation with a lady. I also added that you should never be economical with or embellish the truth when asked about what you do for a living – no matter how tempted you may be. It's true that a lot of women conjure up fantasy images of men employed in certain professions. This can only cause the average Joe in the street to abandon these rules completely and hype up his title in an attempt to compete with these television and media love gods. Typical male stereotypes can be soldiers – all macho rough and dirty, firemen risking life and limb to save damsels (more like cats these days though) in distress together with cool in a crisis, crisp-coated medics who are all square jawed with comforting bedside manners as seen on our screens almost daily from some blood soaked American emergency room format TV show.

While it's true that women go all gooey at the sight of these he-men, what of someone whose occupation is a little less glamorous, such as a dustman or a factory worker? The lure of greasy overalls, grime-encrusted fingers and a guided tour round your lathe just don't seem to carry the same air of excitement now do they?

Well, I'm here to tell all of you out there who have what I would call 'normal' jobs that there's no need to worry. There is definitely no need to hang around burning buildings or your local A&E department as there are numerous other props you can use to attract a woman to great effect. I used some of these props to great success when I was working in 'normal' occupations like as a hotel porter, stock room assistant and yes, believe it or not a dustman. Have faith, be honest and you will be rewarded.

KIDDIES

Women just love babies and I throw down a gauntlet and invite anyone to prove otherwise. I mean it's obvious, otherwise why would young girls just out of school with a future ahead of them as inviting as a criminal serving a 30-year stretch bother having one in the first place? These noisy little bundles of water, wind and vomit are irresistible to the fairer sex and, if they're attached by a hand to a decent looking bloke, one who looks all caring and paternal, then he becomes an instant, straight out of the wrapper, fanny magnet.

I found this out for myself on one occasion whilst minding my mate's two-year-old son. I had taken him to the park for a kick-about and after half an hour, sweating and panting from the exertion (me not him, he was as fresh as a daisy wanting to play longer) we went onto a little cafe for a cooling drink. Talk about flies round a honey pot. Within fifteen minutes I had at least three ladies approach me asking if the little cute bundle of fun was mine and what was his name? It ended up with the little fella drifting off to sleep in my arms, leaving me undisturbed to chat-up his admirer and come away with her number and the promise of a date. However, before you start doing the rounds of friends and relatives begging the loan of a youngster (much to their amazement as since he was born you've never once remembered his birthday or Christmas) there are a number of very important rules to consider. Before hoisting that real-life and bloody heavy Cabbage Patch doll on to your shoulders, make sure you choose an absolute angel of a child. Forget to do this and the sight of you shouting at them louder than a town crier will not endear you to the assembled mass of watching females one bit. They'll just assume you are some bully who can't hold his temper, picks on people much smaller than you and you'll be right back to square one.

Secondly, make sure they like you. If they appear to dote on you and gaze up all puppy eyed as you rock them to sleep then women will do the same. This is relatively easy to achieve and requires only a steady and unlimited supply of sweets, ice cream, toys and other shiny treats. Children are notoriously fickle creatures who will swear allegiance to almost anyone, well at least until the wrapper of the sweet they are eating is licked clean.

To summarise, the answer is as simple as a pocket full of Smarties, a toy car in your hand, a wallet full of wet ones and a smile. Pick them up, shove them under your arm and march into the local park or high street and you'll soon have women following you like the women on the Lynx advert. If you're an orphan and you're friends are all childless then don't despair, here are a couple of other props you can use.

Who was it who said 'diamonds are a girl's best friend'?

FLOWERS

To impress a woman the most important thing you need to do is to make her feel special. There are a million and one ways to do this, but doing so can cost you a fortune. However, a much cheaper though no less efficient method – flowers. Giving flowers to your mother or any other woman you know is easy, but a little bit of ingenuity is called for when offering blooms to someone you've only just met.

Get yourself a bunch from your local florist, remembering the golden rule that the better the flowers, the better the result. For example, a dozen red roses nicely wrapped with a classy bow should net you a girl to match – tall, classily attired and topped off with a red inviting smile. Similarly, a wilting bunch of thirsty carnations hastily grabbed from the forecourt of your local Esso station will see you saddled with a woman who dresses as hastily, eats pies and smells of petrol. Always buy the best you can afford.

Armed with your purchase, begin walking down the street as if you're just out shopping. Smile and walk confidently, catching people's eyes. I guarantee that within minutes some attractive lady is bound to offer you the following comment 'Ooh, are they for me they're lovely?' If she's not to your taste then just smile sweetly, apologise and say that they're for your sick mum and keep on walking. On the other hand, if she's a cracker then smile, reply 'Actually they are' and thrust them into her suprised but grateful feminine grasp.

She will be shocked but also pleased. Now you've got her attention, continue the conversation, again using the conversation and flirting techniques mentioned earlier and get her number or ask her out. I discovered this ploy completely by accident many years ago. I'd just bought my mum a nice big bunch for Mother's day when this gorgeous lady asked if they were for her. I was taken aback by this comment but reacted quickly, said 'yes' and gave them to her. Within minutes, using the excuse that I was in a rush to see my old mum (which was true) I managed to get her number and was just able to nip back into the florist's to buy a second bunch to give to my mum before they closed.

PUPPIES

I think it's true to say that everyone of us would be lying if we didn't admit that we hadn't sat in front of the television all gooey-eyed at the sight of that honey-coloured bundle of fluff as he gets up to all kinds of mischief wrapped in 27 feet of perforated toilet roll. Women are no different. In fact, they're a damn sight worse than we are. Therefore if you find it impossible to prise your sweet-eating, fizzy-drink-guzzling two-year-old nephew from his copy of Grand Theft Auto, the answer is to get yourself a puppy.

If you don't have one yourself already and a phone box makes your flat look spacious, then borrow one from a friend or relative. Even better, advertise yourself as a dog walker and make some much-needed cash. However, if you do go down the purchase route, let me offer you a warning – like credit card debts – puppies grow and grow. – Unlike a storecard that can be paid off early, a puppy is for life, not just for Christmas.

As with the kiddie in the previous section, a walk in the park with this yappy little chappie is guaranteed to get you a larger following than your local HSBC cashpoint spewing out free money. As before you will appear all sensitive and caring and women will be queuing up to stroke it. The younger and more attractive the puppy the better. While they are petting the furry little chap, you have a captivated audience so start the conversation and take it from there.

Whilst walking your puppy it is inevitable that you'll meet someone nice also walking their own dog. This gives you an ideal opportunity to speak to her, as you have something in common to start up a conversation.

If you fluff it or don't pluck up the courage the first time, smile and make a note of what day and time it is, which direction she comes from and whether she walks or drives. Make sure you're about the same time the next day then when you see her again, smile, say 'hello' and then lead (get it, lead) with an open question that is 'doggie based'. Wait for her to respond, use the techniques in the book and success is inevitable. Using this tip it really is that easy to become a love GOD. All you need do is reverse the letters to get DOG. You'd be barking not to!

CLIPBOARD AND PEN

I know of only two acceptable ways for a man to stop a complete female stranger in the street without her yelling out for the Pplice. One is by calling "Big Issue please madam" as she walks by. The other is by holding a clipboard and pen and asking if she minds answering some questions 'that will only take a minute'.

Admittedly the first option may result in a couple of quid or a can of meatychunks for your dog, but the second is more likely to lead to something a little more long term and of a sexual nature. Getting a job as a market researcher is a doddle and need not require a long-term commitment so there's no need to give up your day job. Just browse your local newspaper to see adverts galore from companies specialising in this type of service, all of them looking for someone with a couple of hours to spare and they'll even pay you money for the privilege. (I know it's not exactly top whack, but tell me, when was the last time you got paid to go out on the pull)?

Ring round a couple of companies and ask what type of research they carry out. (By the way, if you do apply you will need to be police checked) Choose a company that targets women's opinions, with subjects like perfume, cat food and alcohol being ideal, but items like detergent and more 'middle aged' subjects, not scoring so well). When you have got the job, simply stand on the street, smile and approach as many pretty girls as possible. Go through your pre-prepared routine, asking her all the relevant questions and at the same time using the conversation and body language techniques detailed earlier. If you find you're getting on well, odds on she'll stay talking for longer than necessary, answer questions not found on your sheet and she may even add her mobile number to the details at the bottom of your form for your eyes only.

///**RULES OF ATTRACTION**//

Don't forget to try combining a wink with a smile in situations where you are getting some positive interest from a woman. Together the actions strongly signal you share her interest.

CHAPTER EIGHT:
LOCATION, LOCATION

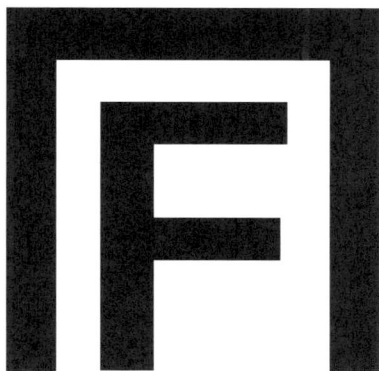

It's not what you do, it's where you do it

As I mentioned previously, pubs, wine bars and nightclubs are just a few of the places available to practice your skills in the art of attraction. Women can be found everywhere, with a number of the most unlikely venues heralding a vast selection of female fruit just ripe for the picking. I've listed just a few of these locations below, together with specific techniques that can be employed in them to full effect.

CAFÉS AND RESTAURANTS

Most waitresses and other female staff who work in these types of establishments are usually experienced and wary of being hit upon by male customers. They are extremely adept at defending themselves from over amorous advances. Techniques to look out for are the 'accidental' emptying of a steaming hot pot of coffee into the unfortunate male's lap or some swift verbal put down, deliberately loud enough for the other customers to hear and relish.

If you want to be successful in these establishments, the trick is to employ an altogether different – and for the recipient – novel approach. One way I found that works a treat is to, apart from when the obligatory 'thank you' is required, not say a word until the time comes to settle the bill. This approach is different from what she's normally used to as most guys when trying to pull her, will continually make what they feel are witty and clever comments. They continually do so when she's taking their order, bringing them their food and even when she's just simply walking past, but you're totally different. Don't say anything but make sure you catch her eye and smile as she carries on working. Then, after you've finished your meal and the time comes to go, leave her a generous tip, look her straight in the eye, smile and say something like 'You really work hard, you deserve this' and then leave.

She'll be pleased at hearing this statement as it proves you've noticed her. Unlike corny and sexual comments, not in a deliberately lecherous way. This compliment, coupled with your controlled exit and her inability

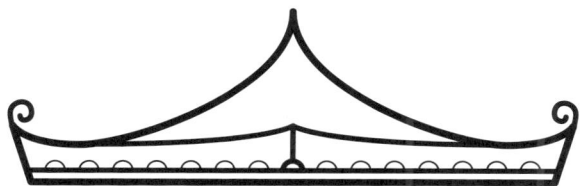

Lemon Grass Restaurant

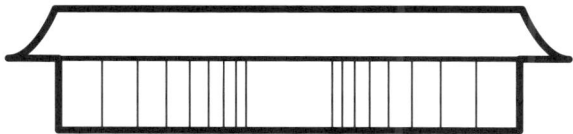

Location, location, location! Use the information she gave you when you met to choose the best place to eat

to respond, will intrigue and leave her looking forward eagerly to your next visit. Never say something corny and definitely never mention her figure, as she'll have you down for some kind of pervert.

Like the phone call to arrange the first date, leave it a couple of days till you return, firstly making sure she's on duty. On entering she should ignore all the other customers and make a beeline for your table to wait on you. This is when you increase your effort, get her talking and then make your move.

I personally last used the same technique to great effect in a wine bar in Doncaster. The waitress, a tall pony-tailed brunette, was working extremely hard serving customers while at the same time trying to fend off the unwelcome advances from a group of city types sat drinking in the corner. Now, I know for a fact that women with long hair only put their hair up into a pony tail or bun when they haven't the time or the inclination to wash and style it. By doing this they make the best of their appearance from a bad situation, although they still don't really feel at their most confident.

I thought I would use this to my advantage so, as I paid for my meal, I left a generous tip, smiled and said 'You have beautiful hair.' I smiled again and then left. She looked stunned, but as I walked out of the door I turned back to show I was interested and she flashed me a great big smile with that gorgeous mouth of hers. I was returning to Doncaster to do a show a few days later, so I popped in for breakfast. She immediately recognized me and came over. We started chatting and the upshot was that I got her number. I saw her quite a few times after that when I was in the area.

Try this for yourself and I'm sure you'll be surprised. Compliment her

///**RULES OF ATTRACTION**//

Never commit her telephone number to memory alone. If you cannot remember it, all your hard work will have been for nothing.

work or choose a body part that she may not feel too good about, steering clear of the obvious ones she's heard more times than Slade's "Merry Xmas Everybody". Don't be like the rest and you are bound to get what the rest are not getting!

HEALTH CLUBS AND GYMNASIUMS

As a bodybuilder these places rank amongst my personal favourites for pulling women. They are full of nubile flesh squeezed into figure-hugging lycra, all sweaty and tousle-haired in their common goal to achieve the perfect body. However, like the bar and restaurant examples above, there are numerous mistakes to be made in these establishments so tread carefully otherwise you may find yourself massaging more than a bruised ego. Here are a few dos and don'ts you should take heed of.

Do:

- Speak to her at the water fountain while she's taking a well-earned rest, allowing her as the gentleman you are to take her turn in front of you. Ask her how long she's been training and then remark that she looks like she really knows what she is doing.
- Take up a position at the treadmill/stepper/cycle/cross trainer next to the one she is using. Most women in these type of places tend to concentrate on cardio so she will be a captive audience for at least ten minutes, during which you can build up a rapport.
- After making sure there are no instructors available, ask her to explain a piece of equipment you say you haven't used before and you've seen her using, She'll fall for the helpless male specimen (as long as you don't ask her to lift up weights for you). After you get to know her better, you could always suggest working out together in and out of the club.
- Join in on one of the exercise classes advertised and get chatting during the floor exercises (if you can manage to speak, that is) then suggest a cool drink at the juice bar afterwards.
- Wear fitted underwear under your gym gear. A friend of mine was exercising at the pec deck at his club when he saw a female member

staring at him mouth agape. He thought she was impressed with the weight he was using. She wasn't. The only reason she was staring was his rather generous legged shorts had ridden up just around his seventh repetition to reveal his love muscle dangling for everyone to see (and it was not pumped).

Don't:

· Try and show off by using too much weight. She won't be impressed, and it's her you want to pull, not a muscle.

· Sweat all over the machine you're using and not wipe it down afterwards. It's impolite gym behaviour and won't endear you to either her or the 18 stone hulk who happens to follow you onto the machine.

· Talk to her while she's in the middle of exercising (apart from cardio). You will only succeed in making her irritable. She may even suffer an injury and so will you if you don't duck as she throws that dumbbell at you.

· Dress in skin-tight luminous Lycra covered in so many labels you look like you've rolled on sport shop's changing room floor. Women will want to be able to see you and what you have to offer, not Versace, Reebok and Nike. Make sure the stuff you wear is comfortable and shows your physique to its best advantage. Therefore ditch the cycling shorts if your legs resemble Grandad's old pipe cleaners.

· Stand in a group with your mates leering and pointing. It may have taken her all of her confidence to join the gym in the first place. Your amateur laddish behaviour will only serve to send her for an early bath – and no, they are not mixed.

· I've been told on many occasions that as a bodybuilder it must have been easy for me to pull, especially in a gymnasium/health club environment. This was not true as my physique actually acted to my disadvantage and I had to use my wits and the above techniques even more when trying to pull. This was because although I had a great body, the majority of women felt shy about approaching me as they felt overawed and intimidated. Yes they all looked, but on so many occasions they ignored me and went off to talk to the weedy guy.

Concentrate on the dos, avoid the don'ts and you may get some one on one personal training.

IT'S QUICKER BY TRAIN

Train and tube carriages packed with hot, sweaty, high-ticket-price-paying, unhappy customers, are not necessarily venues you would immediately associate with encouraging social intercourse.

Sitting (though when was the last time that happened) or standing squashed together closer than applicants for a vacancy in a NHS dentist's waiting room means traveller's individual's personal space is not just invaded, it's positively pillaged. This puts everyone on edge. Therefore even the most polite of approaches is usually met with a put down swifter than if Michael Johnson had qualified as a vet.

To make any headway in this tough location, a radically different approach will be required. In the past I have tried a number of techniques and have been rewarded by some and left red-faced by others. Take advantage of my mistakes and share in the ones that bore fruit.

The first is to attempt to read – without her noticing, of course – what it is she's so engrossed in to the exclusion of all others. The easiest way is to simply read the summary on the back cover of the book. Then quickly Google the author's name to find out a little bit of background history, such as what he or she has written or what's coming out soon from their literary stable. When she takes a break, catch her eye and smile and start the conversation flowing with a relevant question about that particular subject or author. Mention that you've been meaning to read some of their work but have never got around to it. Ask how she's enjoying it (a phonetic ambiguous phrase) and very soon you will be chatting like old friends.

Another is to get yourself a copy of that morning's crossword and feigning a problem, lean across and ask her if she knows the solution to six across, five letters. This is a favourite of mine and always works. If you are travelling by train, the arrival of a drinks trolley (if it's in service of course) will give you the opportunity to refresh not only her thirst, but also your next line so offer her a coffee. Start to look for positive body language signs and mirroring and take it from there. Make sure you get her number before her stop arrives. Should she not be reading, then there's always the state of the railways to discuss, especially with the numerous and lengthy delays that are now the norm. With leaves on the line or frost on the signals, you'll have what feels like a lifetime in which to get acquainted.

Another opportunity to get her talking is by showing yourself as the gentleman that you are and offering her your seat. Even in these days of equality, where women demand the same salaries as men, they secretly enjoy when a man shows his chivalrous side by opening doors and walking on the pavement between her and the road. Therefore smile, get up off that butt and offer her your seat. You never know, get talking and it may not be too long before she's offering you something else.

If she gets on during your regular journey and the train is too packed to be able to speak to her, smile and then make a mental note of the time and day and where she got on and gets off. Most of us are creatures of habit, especially where our working life is concerned so there's a good chance the opportunity will arise again. Armed with her timings, you'll know exactly how long she'll be a captive audience. If you do see her and the train is not too busy, then try and keep a seat next to you so she can sit down. Hopefully she's remembered you from before but if not never fear just smile and start a conversation. Help with her case if she has one, and try to get a sneaky peek at her luggage tag as knowing her name this early on is definitely to your advantage. Let the train take the strain and you never know, it might just be the ticket.

SHOPS, STORES AND SUPERMARKETS

Women love shopping. Supermarkets, shops, stores and the like are full to bursting with women looking for a man – and not just the female store detective hunting that bloke with what looks like a frozen turkey down his trousers.

Different types of approach are required for your fellow shoppers as opposed to female staff, but the end results are exactly the same – you

///**RULES OF ATTRACTION**//

'Who Dares Wins'. Three seconds to make your move, otherwise she may move on or someone else will get in first.

WDW

make your selection from all the tempting goodies and get to carry it home and enjoy it.

Let's start with the female staff member who I feel are the most receptive to an approach. Checkout girls can normally be spotted filing their nails and gossiping about the latest EastEnders depressing storyline or what they're going to wear out on Friday, bored out of their minds with their repetitive chosen occupation. This and the fact that they can't move away when you're talking to them make them prime targets for even the most amateurish men out on the pull. However, before uttering even one word, you must choose the items to be placed on her conveyor belt very very carefully. Research by psychiatrists shows that a lot can be said by what someone puts in their shopping basket. Although not qualified, years of swiping bar codes enables Tracy on the till to deduce the type of person you are just by swiping your sausage and packing your plums. Let me give you an example:

A friend of mine was 'between girlfriends' (as he put it) and popped into his local Tesco's one evening to get his weekly shop. He was paying for his goods when the checkout girl looked up and asked if he was single. Sensing an imminent result he asked 'Is it because I'm buying all these ready-made microwave meals for one?' 'No' she said with a sneer, 'It's because you're ugly!' The moral? Select with care and watch what you're putting in your basket.

As she's swiping your goods, make a mental note of her name from her badge, as it will come in useful. Then start the conversation remembering to always use an open question. As she probably rarely gets a decent conversation during her eight-hour shift, it does not need to be clever. You can replicate the advice given for pulling in a restaurant, but obviously leaving out the bit about the tip. Although not a question, there was one thing I always used to say that never failed me. When the cashier asked if I needed a hand with my packing I replied 'I'm fine, thanks, but I could do with some help paying'. This always got them smiling and I continued from there on. A word of warning though, make sure to keep your chat to a minimum, especially if the store is busy. The last thing you want is a queue forming and risk her getting a rollocking from her supervisor whilst you one from the white-haired old granny who's been waiting ages just to buy a tin of cat food.

When the time comes to pay there's another fantastic tip to test if she's interested. In this day and age plastic is all the rage, but for this experiment hard cash is the preferred currency. Hand her the money and then see what happens next. If she puts your change on the counter for you to pick up without looking then she is not really interested in being picked up herself – it's that simple. However, if she gives you your coins and lingers flesh on flesh, whilst looking straight into your eyes then there's a good chance your going to get more than your loyalty card swiped. Smile back, maybe couple it with a wink, then leave and take your purchases with you. As with the 'train' advice, remember to make a mental note of the time and day. Checkout girls usually work to regular shift patterns, so it's odds on she'll be seated at till three again, same time next week, making it easy for you to work more of your magic.

When you go back next time, get her to serve you again. You can always utilize the technique detailed in the 'groundwork' chapter of this book by standing and surveying the lines of tills. When she looks up and sees you, walk over and deposit your goods on her conveyor belt. This will tell her that out of everyone who is available to serve you, it was her you chose. Say 'hello' then work your magic on her further. I guarantee that by the third visit (you should ask her out on this one, otherwise she may lose interest) she'll be eager to say 'yes' to anything you have on special offer.

These techniques are suitable for checkout girls but also work for any other female staff member. However, now it's time to concentrate on female shoppers. A great way to attract this species is to take advantage of, and play on, the deep maternal instinct they all possess. The way to do this is to amble over to the deli counter. Take your turn in the queue, ask the lady you fancy, the one in front, if she can recommend a particular cheese or ingredient on offer as you're looking to try something new and you really need some advice.

Tell her you're not the naked chef, but could be tempted. As women have a failing for the butter-wouldn't-melt, little-boy-lost look, she will be only too happy to spend some time with you and explain how to tenderize your aubergines. In return and by way of a thank you, offer to treat her to a coffee from the in-store cafe so she can impart more of her culinary expertise and you can get to know her better.

Another great way to start a conversation is when waiting in the queue. Work your charm on the shopper next to you in line. Like trains, the often slow service at supermarket tills affords you plenty of time to engage female customers in conversation. You could try by sharing with her the fact that nine per cent of our time is spent standing in queues or by asking about some unique item nestling in her basket. The technique is always the same. The question should be open, prompting more than a single word reply, relevant and coupled with positive and open body language.

Alternatively, as you meet her in the aisle, lightly bump trolleys, smile, apologize and insist that you exchange personal details for insurance purposes as you may well want to sue for whiplash. This one is guaranteed to get a giggle. By way of a further apology you can always offer to help with her shopping as we have covered previously, women still love a gentleman.

These specific pick-up tricks, together with all the other techniques contained in this book, can be applied to many different venues and will work equally well at them all. Choose your venue carefully as the type of establishment you go to pull, dictates the type of women who frequents it. If you want to meet a posh shopper then you have to forego Kwik Save for Claridge's – although after glimpsing your till receipt you may well be forced to choose somewhere less expensive in future.

CHAPTER NINE:
THE FIRST DATE

The time's come – don't blow it

After you've called her up and arranged the date, it's time to consider two important issues – the way you are going to look and how you are going to dress. Now's the ideal time to invest some money and effort to ensure you look your best so step up your pre-date grooming regime to the max.

If you've a few days spare before the date then get your hair trimmed, invest in a manicure and even go as far as treating yourself to a mini facial to ensure you look spot on. However, never have this type of treatment the day before the date as your skin can sometimes de-toxicate and as a result, you may wake up on the day with a pimple or two ready to rival Vesuvius in the eruption stakes.

Next, think carefully about exactly what you're going to wear. I certainly don't need to tell you that jeans to the opera or a tuxedo to the pub are likely to raise more than her eyebrows, Careful consideration is needed before you make your decision.

Check the venue out if this is the first time you've been and find out if they have a dress code. There's nothing worse than getting there, ready to impress, only to be refused entry because you're not wearing a tie or whatever else the management insist on. If no such restrictions apply then look to see what the other guys are wearing and dress accordingly.

The chosen venue should have been agreed by you both, but if she has left the choice entirely yours then avoid like the plague your local haunts, as she won't be too enamoured to meet your grinning mates this early in your 'relationship', and will definitely not want to be confronted by your ex of two weeks' standing, spitting venom like some hooded she-cobra. A nice restaurant is a safe bet, one not too flash. Remember to use all of

///**RULES OF ATTRACTION**//

Gaze – never stare at a woman. If she returns you gaze, look away as if searching for someone else before returning you gaze to her. If she looks away and then looks at you again then she is interested.

▷4

the information gained when speaking to her the other evening regarding food likes and dislikes before making your choice. This pre-date detective work will help avoid you witnessing her total horror and disgust when you turn up arm in arm at Bernie's Big Grill only to discover that she is a committed vegan.

As far as the actual date is concerned, the timing of you your arrival can be likened to your performance between the sheets. Making her wait will only end up with her getting bored and possibly leaving before you even get there. Arriving too early just smacks of desperation and lack of control. As women are notoriously bad timekeepers and the last thing you want if it's cold is mild hypothermia, park somewhere close to the venue where you can see her arrival in comfort. When you see her coming, jump out of the car and stroll up just behind her. Smile, say 'Hi' and apologise for being late (although you weren't really). The calculating and competitive creature she is will be slightly disappointed that you've beaten her at her own game so early on, but secretly pleased too that you've shown yourself as a man who's in control of the situation.

To prevent having to spend the whole evening with her should she look different from when you met, turn out to be duller than the undercoat on your kit car project or is starting to talk about how she's always wanted to be married and raise a large family, you really should have a get out of jail free card handy. Here's one I used to use all of the time. Ask a friend to call you on your mobile at a pre-arranged time, say an hour after you've arranged to meet her. If you're going to the cinema then he should send a text with your phone on silent mode to avoid pissing off the rest of the fee-paying public. Ask him to let you know that there's a problem at work that only you can solve then you can offer your apologies and leave. However, if she looks more delectable than the night you met or is promising to get into positions you only thought yoga instructors could manage then explain to your mate that you're way too busy and tell him not to wait up.

As you've done most of the hard work before asking her out, again remember the rules of conversation and flirting, but this time you can relax a little and take things a little further.

If you chose the cinema as your venue, then take her for a drink afterwards to discuss the film. Again, make note of her reactions to your open questions and her body language. A lot of people liken the cinema for a first date venue to a brewery for a meeting of the AA – after all, it's not exactly a place where conversation is encouraged. This may be so, but if this is where she wants to go then live with it. The cinema does have some advantages. Seated in the warmth and near darkness of gives you oodles of opportunity to check her out without her noticing. It also provides the added opportunity to enjoy close physical proximity without the need for an excuse.

Let's turn the clock forward a couple of hours. The film's credits have long since rolled or the plate has been licked clean in the Little Chef (only joking). Now you are both sat in the pub, getting on like a house on fire (why do they say that?)

Remember to offer to pay for everything, but whatever happens, do not start coming over all domineering and aggressive if she insists on paying her share, just let her. She may want to show her independence, especially in this day and age where women earn as much as men. She may not want to feel she owes you anything, as she might have had experience of guys in the past who, just because they've bought her three Bacardi Breezers, see it as their God-given right to expect sexual favours in return. Ever the gent, simply insist that you pay next time and see how she reacts to that forward thinking statement. By now you should be well at the stage where formalities have long since been dispensed with, so it's time to make her feel like she's known you for ages, and not that you met just over a week ago. This is because any woman is far more likely to sleep with someone she feels she already knows well as opposed to a total stranger, unless of course she's a female escort.

The technique I'm now going to explain is called 'emotional bonding'. It has the powerful effect of putting her in a higher emotional – and therefore even more receptive – state of mind than normal, and one which is more open to your suggestions.

It's a little like hypnosis. You should start to use certain phrases in your

GEORGE AND THE DRAGON

If she does turn out to be a dragon – there are easier ways to get rid of her

conversation, similar to the ones detailed in the 'Groundwork' chapter, that have the effect of playing on her subconscious. These can be as simple as saying you loved the film you just watched together, eating the same foods or using more specific phrases such as:

· We **feel** exactly the same way as each other.
· Isn't that an **amazing** coincidence?
· I've always **felt** like that.
· We really must **do that together.**

When she's reached this emotional 'high' again, it's time to push further in search of your goal. Start to litter your conversation using her name occasionally and the word 'we' more often, when talking about the future. Using her name during the conversation helps her recognize that you are focussing on her alone and the use of the word 'we' helps to forge a strong subliminal bond between the two of you. Start to take the lead in the conversation. As you do, gradually increase these words and insert stronger, more powerful subliminal messages and verbal commands such as:

· Want it
· Do it
· Take it
· Need it
· Use it

Make sure that while using these words in your conversation, you don't deliver them too prominently or in a deliberate sexual context, as this is what you want her to do. By delivering the messages in a seemingly innocent way, it's up to her subconscious to absorb them, analyse and then convert them to convey a deep sexual meaning.

So don't mention sex at all unless of course she does. Instead, let her imagine it through her subconscious being bombarded with all these powerful phonetic ambiguities. She will soon be suggesting it – that's a promise. As the date continues, increase your suggestive phrases even more to help make her succumb even quicker such as:

· Surrender
· Open
· Penetrate
· Come over

Again, remember not to overemphasize these phrases too deliberately. You've been bombarding her with more prompts than a forgetful actor in a West End play, so you're now ready for stage two. Instead of just mentioning single words within sentences or phrases I want you to slowly turn up the pressure even more by combining them within the description of an actual pleasurable physical action. Doing this will bring your date's mental state to an even higher level.

You should still have the information stored from your initial meeting, so choose something she mentioned that she really adored. If it was a particularly enjoyable holiday location, then bring the conversation around to that subject again. Start to describe in detail, all the pleasurable things that could happen in this scenario. Begin by mentioning her lying on a white fine sandy beach, the sun hot on her body and the clear turquoise water gently lapping her toes. Then progress further by describing the action of firm hands massaging sun cream into her bare flesh.

If she mentioned previously that she just adores Belgian chocolates, then again turn the conversation around to this subject. Start talking her through choosing one, the look, the shape, and the texture. Progress to describing how the chocolate smells, the intense feeling as her tongue experiences it's coolness and then the sensation of biting into it. Describe it feeling creamy and delicious, swirling round on her tongue before she swallows. Now ask her to imagine a similar scenario and instead of you describing it ask her to describe it to you herself. As she does so you'll immediately notice her face start to flush with excitement, her eyes widen. She will be in such a highly charged state sexually and emotionally that she'll soon be putty in your hands.

It's now time to cut the evening at the bar short and suggest a nightcap back at either hers or yours and get ready for the fireworks. If however she still isn't ready to succumb, then don't despair, as Rome wasn't built in a day (Redditch was, though). If you have got this far without an imprint of her palm across your cheek, then you've obviously made a favourable impression and with a little more work next time, you're bound to get a result.

As you walk or drive her home, seal all that hard work with a kiss. I find it amazing how many guys who do everything spot on right up to this stage only spoil it all by sucking her face off like an industrial strength Dyson. Like shaving, kissing takes loads of practice to get it right. Again like shaving we have to discover for ourselves how to do it correctly as there's no-one around to show us how. I can vividly remember my own initiation into the art of kissing. Mortified as I am to reveal it, hope you find it funny (but hopefully not half as painful as I did) and learn from it.

I was about 11-years-old, had just been prescribed Joe 90 glasses to combat being short sighted and had recently discovered girls. I was a virgin in more ways than one, never even having kissed a girl. I decided to share my problem with my elder brother, hoping to get some tips. Listening intently, he pointed out that the solution to my problem lay with the bathroom mirror. Like other boys my age I would admit to having spent many a happy evening squeezing facial spots till they erupted like a volcano all over the glass. However, for the life of me was at a loss to fathom how this practical, but ultimately inanimate household object could help me in my pubescent plight. My brother sighed and explained that the best way to practice was by using the mirror almost as a surrogate female. This way he explained, I could practice my 'snogging' as he put it in complete privacy and also examine my technique at the same time. He was my big brother so I believed him, well you would wouldn't you? I immediately dashed off to the bathroom to start

///**RULES OF ATTRACTION**//

First impressions count. You only have up to 10 seconds from when she first sees you till when she is likely to look away. Make the most of that short time to catch her eye in a postive way.

puckering up. Sure it was cold and felt weird at first, but I felt that I was starting to get the hang of it when whack! The door pushed open and my face exploded all over the mirror in a torrent of blood, chipped teeth and broken glass. I was to find out later, following a trip to the local hospital, that my elder brother had in fact paid my younger brother the princely sum of 25 pence (pre-decimalisation weekly pocket money) to give the door a kick. I did get my own back in a non-violent way though by drawing bikinis on his *Playboy* nudes in permanent marker.

As you can see there are more pitfalls with kissing than in a Welsh miner's photo album. Take note and hopefully you'll be guaranteed not to trip up. The most singularly important piece of advice I can share is that when moving in for the kiss, let the lady take the lead and set the pace. This is because people generally like to kiss someone in exactly the same way they like to be kissed themselves. Don't go charging off like a 100 metre Olympian, instead adopt the mindset of the marathon runner, allowing her to run on ahead and then following on with more of what she does. Also notice where she puts her hands, as this will give you an indication of where best to put yours. Judge the strength of her kisses and whether or not she used her tongue. Again as before, let her take the lead and then play catch up.

The best type of practice for kissing is to do it as much as possible, (and not in a mirror). Make a firm second date and remember that even the pied piper started with just one rat following him. Before you know it you'll have her and even more just like her following you.

APPENDIX

Anatomy of
a great puller

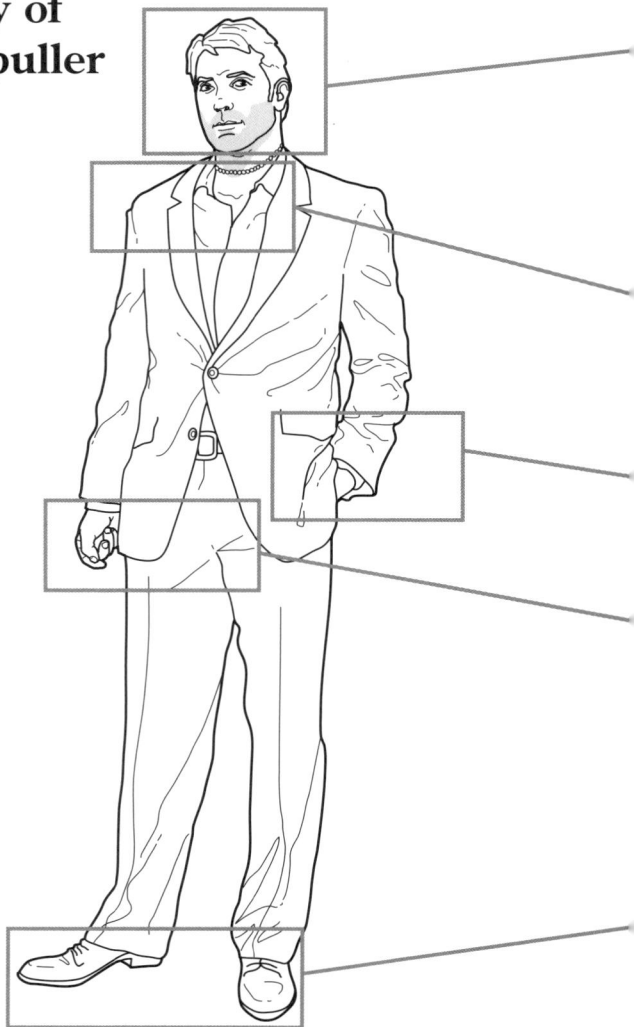

- **Head tilted to one side and pointing towards 'target'.**
- **Eyebrows raised to advertise interest.**
- **Gaze, don't stare, look at her, then away, then back again. Increase rate of blinking or look for mirroring.**
- **Smile.**
- **Mirror her actions but not straight away. Wait 30 seconds.**
- **Stand tall – don't slouch but do relax.**
- **Body facing 'target' and groin slightly forward. Lean in slightly towards 'target' but watch out for her no-go zone!**
- **Hands on hips shows confidence and physical prowess. Tuck thumb into pocket and splay fingers pointing to genitals Hands and wrists open denote honesty.**
- **Hand behind head displays armpit (erogenous zone) or play with hair. If you have none, softly rub your head. She may just follow your lead.**
- **Choose jewellery to reflect personality – bling, surfer dude.**
- **Legs apart to accentuate groin. Knees relaxed and pointing at 'target'.**
- **Feet pointing at 'target'. Try lightly touching her foot with yours – see if she moves away.**

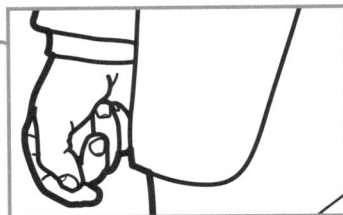

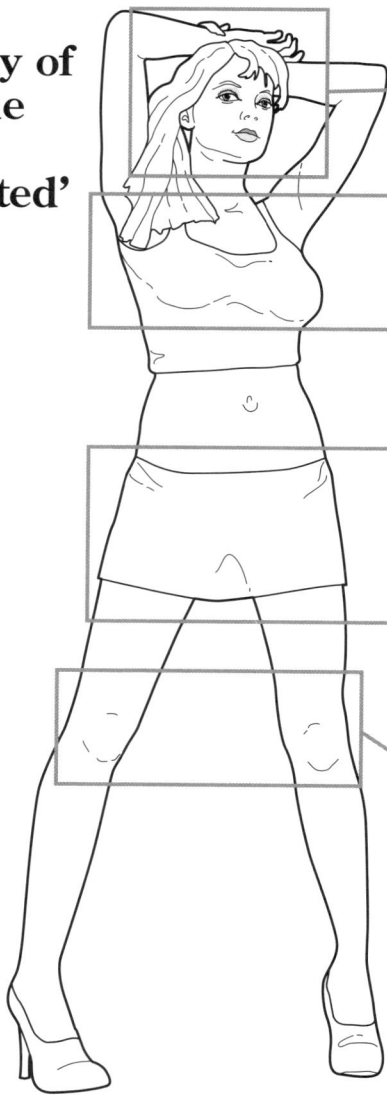

Anatomy of someone who's 'interested'

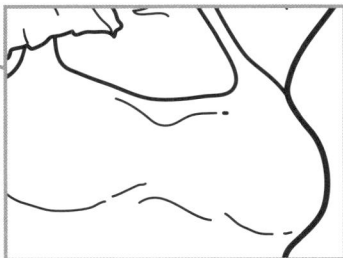

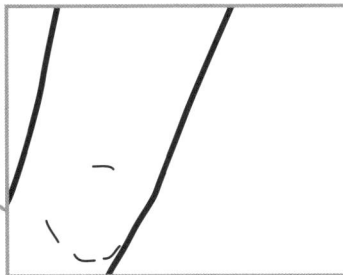

- Hair: touching, smoothing, playing with it. She's saying 'look at me'.
- Eyebrows raised.
- Eyes: large pupils shiny, sparklingly and keep looking at your mouth (or groin).
- Hands, playing with bottle neck or glass.
- Wrists exposed.
- Mouth: licking lips, tongue between teeth, nibbling on pens, straws, etc.
- Shoulders shrugged on initial meeting.
- Arms outstretched towards you.
- Clothes: look for undone top buttons or glimpses of flesh. Body leans in towards you.
- Bum: if she smooths it so you can see, she's saying 'please look'.
- Legs: lots of good signals here. If sitting she:

a) crosses them, foot pointing towards you.
b) keeps crossing and uncrossing.
c) leaves one leg with foot twisted behind around calf or ankle
d) lets her shoe dangle off her foot.

Room scenarios

TOILETS

Good positioning – by the bar

Standing with your back to the bar means you get a great view of the whole of the room to suss out who's there and who you're interested in. You can also chat up the bar maid when she's not busy (don't forget to tip her well so when you are talking to a lady and order a drink you'll get preferential treatment). Today's independent and liberated women actually buy their own drinks so they will actually come to you, halving the work you need to do to strike up that winning conversation.

However, don't slouch or stand in the same place too long otherwise everyone will think you're an alcoholic and give you a berth wider than P&O's new super liner.

Good positioning – entrance

By framing yourself in the doorway for a minute everyone in the room gets a good look at you. If you are looking your best and standing confidently, you will create a great first impression. Look round the room as if you're looking for someone (whilst making a mental note where the attractive women are for later) then make your way in confidently to your chosen spot always passing through the centre of the room first.

However, don't do what a mate of mine did. He stood in the doorway for far too long, milking his entrance so the bouncers got impatient and almost pushed him into the room. This threw him completely, he lost his bearings and headed for the loos.

Disaster struck when instead of the gents, he opened the wrong door and walked into the general store cupboard where all the toilet cleaning materials were kept.

He stayed in there red-faced and sweating for a whole 25 minutes while everyone awaited his embarrassed exit. When he did come out he must have covered the distance between the hastily opened door and his car outside in a time to rival Olympic 100 metre finalists.

Good positioning – part of a group

Standing as part of a group who are enjoying themselves is a great place to position yourself. Women adore guys who are having a good time as they presume that they are fun to be around and could show them a good time too.

Position yourself on the edge of the group. Here you are able to continue to dip into the safety of the group when required but also make yourself available to others. In this position you can turn your body towards women who interest you and play a tantalising game of flirting 'peek-a-boo'. You do this by making initial eye contact then breaking it by rejoining the group and talking to someone else or joining in with a joke. Just when they think you're not interested, hit them with a full on smile and beckon them over to join you, making a space or leaving the group to join them.

Bad positioning – middle of a group

Being part of a group has its benefits whilst trying to pull the fairer sex. However, position yourself incorrectly and what initially turned out to be to your advantage before you know it quickly flips around and kicks you on your bum. Standing too close to the centre of the group only serves to prevent you from taking advantage of all your newly acquired pulling skills. You can't see out to make eye contact with anyone, your positive body language is useless (unless hands waving above your head and you jumping up and down is an until now undiscovered positive body language action) and no-one else can see you to do the same.

Even if you do manage to catch the eye of someone you fancy, your position prevents them from easily getting to you and vice versa.

As in football's offside rule, position is everything. Keep on side and you'll be certain to score.

Good positioning – near the toilets

Fact, women go to the toilet in a pub or club more than men. They do this for several reasons. To re-apply their make up, check out the competition in the harsh and unforgiving glare of the ladies loos and also to gain the opinion of their mate as to whether or not the bloke who's been giving her the eye for the past twenty minutes really is interested or has in fact just had both his cataracts done and been told by his GP not to blink for the next 24 hours.

Anyway, standing in the pathway women use to get to the loos is a great place. Make eye contact as they are en route, smile and then look out for them smoothing their jeans or skirts over the bum as they walk past. This is a great positive body language giveaway that says "look at my bum" and "I'm interested". Looking back and smiling is also a positive sign and says "You're cute but you're going to have to make all the running".

Before they come out again, move to a different place and then watch them look for you. They'll be disappointed that they can't see you, and then putty in your hands when you pop up and start talking to them.

Bad positioning – the dance floor

There is one golden rule that must be adhered to. Unless you're closely related to John Travolta's dance teacher then this area of all places is definitely out of bounds.

All too often, hours of hard work and successful preliminary flirting have been destroyed in a matter of seconds. The sight of flailing arms and bandy legs, moving not only against the music but also fellow dancers, can cause angry scenes, bruised shins and egos.

Better to stay within the relative safety and comfort of the carpet and share a laugh with that attractive blonde as you both grasp each other uncontrollably and delight at the dance floor occupants clumsy attempts to do the "Time Warp".

Bad positioning – on your own

Even if the location is a bigger dump than one of King Kong's toilets, standing on your own in a corner of a pub or club trying to pull is not what I consider a good move. You may well be good looking, witty and charming, but standing in a corner, nursing a bottle of Beck's just smacks of desperation. Not just me, but to everyone else watching.

Looking like Billy No-mates also starts to get boring after a while. Boredom affects the way you feel inside and more important, your body language and how you appear to others. Visible signs are slouching, your head drops, and you avoid meeting people's eyes. This image sends out the overwhelming message, "I'm bored, and have no energy" so in turn, people avoid even looking at you.

The answer is to bring a friend with you or if you're in a strange place either get chatting to the barman or the bouncers so at least you'll have someone to talk to. Alternatively, pretend you're waiting for a mate and approach someone you fancy quickly. Tell them you can't talk for long as you're expecting someone any minute. This approach means they won't feel pressured into talking you all evening as they think you'll be going any minute. Then, when you're getting along like a house on fire, you can invent a text message from your mate (on silent mode of course) cancelling the meeting, thus freeing you up to carry on the good work with the lady.

Bad positioning – tight group of women

Approaching a tight knit group of women will guarantee you end up with more than a flea in your ear and something extremely sore down your trousers.Women standing talking together are a formidable bunch and harder to break into than Fort Knox so avoid this scenario if you can. If you enjoy a challenge and must persist then look out for some important signs and bide your time.

Look for one of the group slowly edging away from their friends and looking around the room. This says that they are not as interested in being part of the pack any more, and with some teasing may be tempted to leave the safety of the group. Make initial eye contact and see what happens. She will probably look away and return to the safety of the group, but return your gaze after a minute, which says she's interested.

Never, ever approach the group unless invited otherwise the overriding body language signal you'll receive is two fingers outstretched on the end of a dainty wrist. Instead, wait for your target to either break off from the pack to go to the ladies and then do your stuff or the group to break into smaller, less intimidating pieces.

I made all the mistakes so you don't have to.

I really hope that you've enjoyed reading this book and have learnt a lot from it. The pathway to successful attraction is full of pitfalls and obstacles. However, with everything I've shared with you I really believe that you are now better equipped to deal with them and are ready to go out and start living your life to the full.

Remember, this is not a work of fiction, but all based on fact and personal experience. I used all of the techniques mentioned myself and was transformed from a geek to a god. Do yourself a favour, try it and I know that you'll be amazed by the result.

I wish you all the best.

Clive 'RS' Webb